WHAT OTHERS SAY ...

In *Revive Your Life! Rest for Your Anxious Heart*, author Pamela Christian gives us a picture of God's love in a way that will most likely be a game-changer for many. She does so with the skill of an artist and the scholarship of an apologist, yet she writes with the compassionate heart of a pastor. This book illustrates the biblical concept "the truth shall make you free." One translation reads, "you shall know the truth in an experiential way, and the truth shall make you free." That well represents the backbone of this book. It is an invitation to the ongoing experience of truth through a relationship with a perfect heavenly Father. *Revive Your Life!* is a tool that will bring great numbers of people into the freedom they were born for through the discovery of their God-given purpose and significance.

BILL JOHNSON, Bethel Church, Redding, CA, Author of *When Heaven Invades Earth* and *God is Good*

Pamela Christian's *Revive Your Life!* is informative, inspirational, and challenging. This third volume in her highly readable trilogy (following *Examine Your Faith!* and *Renew Your Hope!*) puts some very important truths in the Christian faith on "the bottom shelf" and will be edifying to those seeking truth and to new converts, as well as to those who have walked for many decades with Jesus. While I am in disagreement with the author on the extant nature of some of the spiritual gifts experienced by the first century Church, I would recommend this book to all who seek to know more about the Christian faith.

DR. RICHARD LAND, President, Southern Evangelical Seminary, Charlotte, North Carolina

A well-known song recorded years ago aptly declares, "What the World Needs Now Is Love." This is truer today than when the song broke upon the scene a generation ago. In fact, Jesus Himself warned us that in the "Last Days" the love of many would turn cold! But thank God for people like Pamela Christian who is brave enough to say, "Not on my watch!" *Revive Your Life! Rest for Your Anxious Heart* is truly a manual full of directions on how to rekindle your faith, hope, and love and arise to fulfill your distinct call in this generation. If your heart needs to be revived, then read on. This was written with you in mind."

DR. JAMES W. GOLL, Founder of God Encounters Ministries, International Speaker, Best-Selling Author

Revive Your Life! Rest for Your Anxious Heart is the logical and indispensable conclusion to Pamela Christian's trilogy, *Faith to Live By*. Having established in volume one the historical and objective truths of Holy Scripture—in contrast to the flawed and unsubstantiated claims of non-Christian religions—she leads readers in volume two to experience the hope, rewards, and "breakthroughs" available to all who accept God's promises and the life-changing power of biblical Christianity. In this third volume, Pamela sets out to lead her readers step-by-step through and beyond the deceptions, pitfalls, and other obstacles that the enemies of Christ—both demonic and human—put forth to discourage potential and practicing Christians from embracing a truth-based, God-centered life. But Pamela doesn't stop here. Ultimately, volume three is all about God's love, and how "to enter a transformed life of freedom, joy, and victory" through a genuine, empowered relationship with Jesus Christ. In *Revive Your Life!* Pamela Christian helps her readers embrace a loving relationship with their Creator. She explains how to grow and mature in this relationship, both experientially as well as practically. As a natural result of this, she explains how God's love can play out in each of our lives to impact our sinful, suffering world for Christ. Whether you are a spiritual seeker, a new believer, or a mature Christian facing spiritual struggles and doubts, this book is for you.

DAN STORY, MA Christian Apologetics, Author and Teacher

Pamela Christian has produced another book in her *Faith to Live By* series that will be an encouragement to many. She paints an exciting biblical picture of what it means to be a follower of Christ—and bases it on the very best mix of fact and feeling.

CRAIG J. HAZEN, Ph.D., Professor of Apologetics, Biola University Author of *Five Sacred Crossings*

As a Christian apologist, I so appreciate Pamela's ability to blend heart and head by equipping believers to experience the love and presence of God in a way consistent with God's Word which avoids spiritual deceptions. *Revive Your Life! Rest for Your Anxious Heart* is a must-read for anyone struggling to understand the true nature of God's love through the lens of logical and biblical truth.

BOB DUTKO, Christian Apologist and Nationally Syndicated Christian Talk Show Host

I found *Revive Your Life! Rest for Your Anxious Heart* to be a fresh voice of reason, especially significant for those searching for meaning and purpose in life. Pamela's attention to theological and personal detail is refreshing, engaging, and revitalizing. Whether you are among the four million who are in search of hope, the twenty-one million struggling with depression, or thirty-nine thousand considering suicide, this book will provide answers to your life questions—you will find Jesus is the answer to your desperation and remedy for your despair. Don't just buy one copy of this book. Buy two copies and give one to someone more desperate than you. You won't have to look too far to find someone who needs it.

DR. SHERYL D. GIESBRECHT, Speaker, Radio/TV Personality, Global Influencer, Author of *Experiencing God Through His Names*, www.FromAshesToBeauty.com

In today's culture of confusion and trouble, the subject of "faith" and how to apply it, is greatly needed. Once again, Pamela Christian gives us fresh insights into God's Word, which have been tried and proven in her own life. Pam's heart to help others experience the victorious life available through faith in Christ is one constant theme in all she does. After reading her first two books, I offered to endorse the next book in the series. Through her authentic, practical, and applicable writings you'll learn that the most difficult spots in life can also become the places of new revelation or a new beginning. I am pleased to endorse and recommend this book to both new converts and the seasoned followers of Christ.

DR. ANDREW BILLS, Bishop & Founder of The Holy Spirit Broadcasting TV Network, www.hsbn.tv

I wish I'd had this book back when I was a drifting agnostic. The main thing that drew me to consider the truth claims of Christianity was the realization if there was no God, there was no hope. Any hope I thought I had, would be merely an illusion, and secular humanism was nothing more than wishful thinking—not based on reality. In *Revive Your Life! Rest for Your Anxious Heart,* Pamela Christian's third installment of her *Faith to Live By* series, she very effectively demonstrates how secularism's increase in the West since the period known as the Enlightenment, has not only failed to fulfill our deepest longings, but also utterly fails to explain why we have those longings in the first place! Not only does Pamela present a solid and compelling case that the Christian worldview is the only way the world makes sense, but that the Judeo-Christian God of the Bible is a God of perfect love, justice, mercy, and grace who longs to have an intimate relationship with each one of us. If there is one thing I've learned as someone who works in the field of Christian Apologetics, it's that apologetics is not just about presenting arguments and offering a defense of Christianity; it's about inviting and introducing others to the fulfilled promise of God in the person of Jesus Christ. Pamela Christian gets it right on all counts!

GREG WEST, Founder and editor of The Poached Egg Christian Worldview Apologetics Network, www.ThePoachedEgg.org, and National Leadership team member at Ratio Christi Campus Apologetics Alliance, www.RatioChristi.org.

When you know the truth, it does set you free! (John 8:32). Pamela's latest book in her series *Faith to Live By* skillfully confronts the distortion of truth birthed through deception. The author brilliantly uses her words like a sharp sword to cut away the false to see the unvarnished truth behind the lies of our culture and our hearts. *Revive Your Life!* is a pilgrimage to discover the authentic beauty of the Christian life when truth is the foundation. If life has hit you hard and you find yourself examining all you believe, this book will help you find rest for your anxious heart and strengthen your path.

CYNTHIA CAVANAUGH, Speaker, Life Coach, and author of *Unlocked: 5 Myths Holding Your Influence Captive*, and *Live Unveiled: Freedom to Worship God, Love Other and Tell Your Story.*

Pamela writes for people in need—reaching out not just to the unsaved but also to Christians who need a little push in the right direction. Everyone is in need of prayer, encouragement, and a plan of action. In plain English, we're just all in need! Pam reminds us that our needs are met in one Creator Lord. Only in the God whose Son Jesus came to save us, redeem us, sanctify us, and give us eternal life are we going to find the kind of help that truly meets our needs for now and forever! And only in the Holy Spirit are we empowered to accomplish our goals. Her latest book in her *Faith to Live By* series entitled *Revive Your Life! Rest for Your Anxious Heart* will give you a big head start in the right direction.

JIMMIE HANCOCK, Chaplain, Colonel, USAF, Retired

Revive Your Life!

Rest for Your Anxious Heart

Pamela Christian

Revive Your Life!
Rest for Your Anxious Heart
Book Three in the *Faith to Live By* book series

Pamela Christian's books may be ordered through all fine booksellers or direct through Pamela Christian Ministries:
18032 Lemon Drive #C206
Yorba Linda, CA 92886
www.pamelachristianministries.com

Published by Protocol, Ltd.
info@protocolpublishing.com

ISBN-13: 978-0-9909421-8-4 (sc)
ISBN-10: 0-9909421-8-X (sc)
ISBN-978-06156040-2-2 (hc)
ISBN-13: 978-0-9909421-9-1(e)

Library of Congress Control Number: 2017937202
Printed in the United States of America.

"The steadfast love of the Lord never ceases, his mercies never come to an end; they are new every morning; great is your faithfulness."

Lamentations 3:22

This book, this book series, and my life's work are dedicated to the One who demonstrated His love for me even when I was the most unlovable; dedicated to the One whose love is constant and extended to all who will choose to respond to, and be transformed by, His love. May this book be among the many ways God works to reveal to you He *is* love.

CONTENTS

ACKNOWLEDGMENTS

M_y *Faith to Live By* book series was, without a doubt for me, inspired by God. I was first moved to write when I read an article that revealed how tremendously deceived people are. Filled with both compassion and outrage, I found myself quickly writing *Examine Your Faith! Finding Truth in a World of Lies.* While writing the first book, I sensed deep within me at least two more books would become part of the newly forming series. *Renew Your Hope! Remedy for Personal Breakthroughs* is the second book. And now, *Revive Your Life! Rest for Your Anxious Heart,* completes the series—at least for now.

One person most deserving of public appreciation is Dan Story. I'd read several of his books and never expected to meet him—let alone have him become a most gracious mentor. Dan read my initial manuscript for the first book in this series. In reflection, Dan could have correctly responded by telling me to throw the manuscript away and start over. Instead, Dan gently walked me through the rough spots providing suggestions and encouragement. I'm sure he didn't realize for me that sealed the deal, and he's been involved in each book since. I greatly value his investment in me, and I pray I will continue to produce work that helps others discover and apply the truth to find the victory and abundant life Christ died to provide us.

Another person who has proven indispensable to me as a writer is my editor and dear friend, Deb Haggerty. I have learned a great deal from her, and expect to continue to learn more as she's one of the best editors I've ever worked with. So much so, Deb is the only editor I want to have work with me on my projects.

The cover designer for all three of my books in this series is Lisa Knight. I thoroughly enjoyed working with her, finding the perfect cover images to visually introduce the individual book content, and generating a collection of images that clearly identify the three books as part of the same series. Beyond her talent as a graphic designer, I also greatly value her keen understanding of branding. The imagery for Pamela Christian Ministries is beautiful and much appreciated.

Together, we have worked on the *Faith to Live By* book series project, for the purpose of producing quality content with excellence for you—the readers of my books. The vast majority of you, I have not met. However, you have a special place in my heart because all the ministry work I do is for you. I was graced to discover God and His love, and His love compels me to share what I've found with others. He wants everyone to embrace Him in truth. If you embark on the journey with me, I promise you will discover that God *is* love.

INTRODUCTION

As a retreat and conference speaker, I get to travel to meet many people. Over the past twenty-five years, I have noted that growing numbers of people are utterly dissatisfied with their lives on one or more levels. The failure of government and politics, the demise of marriage and family, the breakdown of job and economic markets, the antagonistic culture and social issues—all are cited as sources of discontent. Seemingly, there isn't an area of our human existence that hasn't been adversely impacted. The result is a profound culture of restlessness and division. Understandably, people are seeking solutions that will reform our society.

People are earnestly seeking remedies out of a desire to be rid of the relentless and contentious anxiety to find rest for their hearts and to find a greater meaning and purpose for their lives.

What about you? As you're reading this book, I can presume you are among those who are in some measure unfulfilled, anxious, and hoping to find meaning and significance for your life. Perhaps you're even hoping to find a compelling foundation upon which to rebuild your life. If so, you are the reason I've written this book.

I came to a point in my life many years ago when I became crushingly aware that everything I'd been building my beliefs on was a progression of lies. My life focus was meaningless, and my life direction would never lead me to my desires for the future. I didn't know where to find the advice and answers I needed. I wasn't even certain a better way existed. But deep within, I had the nagging sense there must be a better way—there must be something greater than what I knew. So, I set out in hopes of finding the meaning and purpose in life that I longed for. *Revive Your Life! Rest for Your*

Anxious Heart puts into words part of the glorious discovery I made then and now seek to share to help others.

My life focus is to help people discover the same life-giving truth I've been blessed to find. The way I most often begin when I'm speaking to a group is to ask all my audiences the same question: "Who in this room wants to live their life on the basis of a lie?" No one ever raises their hand. That fact is exceedingly revealing. Since no one ever raises his or her hand, we can deduce that *universally,* we prefer truth over deception. In other words, we *all* have an innate moral compass, which allows us to distinguish between what is "good" and what is "bad." The next logical question is "If no one *wants* to live their life on the basis of a lie, and since *universally,* we can distinguish between good and bad, why don't *all* people choose what is good and true?" The answer is found in one word: deception.

People are deceived, and they don't know they are because that is the nature of deception—the victim is unaware. Deception is something no one wants, yet I believe the vast majority of people experience. I certainly did. How can people be freed from deception, especially since they are unaware of their condition? By being open to examining what they believe and why they believe what they believe. Unless we intentionally examine our beliefs, we can easily be deceived and not know that we are.

If you are willing to open your mind to consider matters from an unbiased perspective, I believe you will uncover deception has been robbing you of the most fulfilling life of hope, and the promising future that you were meant to have. Consider this: How could we feel *any* sense of insignificance, unless we were created *for* significance?

The very fact you have an undeniable sense there must be more—there must be something better, is evidence that such exists. I believe no one can find true personal fulfillment unless they discover truth and love in the reality of God.

Discovering truth is simple. But, there has been a concerted effort to distort the truth and keep you from the discovery of truth. If you believe you are created, that implies a Creator, which is contrary to the popular concept of *evolution*. If you are a product of the American educational system, you likely believe all that exists came from a great cosmic explosion, followed by the process of *evolution* and survival of the fittest. Evolution does not require a Creator—making humanity the highest evolved of all beings. We will explore evolution further in chapters two and three. If you are open-minded and apply basic logic and reason, you will be led to conclude the truth that God exists and, He created you in His image to live a life of supreme significance. You will learn all that is good and loving comes from the one true God because He *is* love.

Just as there has been a strategic effort to distort our understanding of truth, so there has been an intentional effort to prevent us from knowing God and His *multifaceted love*.

A popular rock group of the sixties and seventies, The Beatles, wrote and sang songs challenging us to imagine a better world—with one song claiming *all we need is love*. Considering all the perversities of wars, evil, and wickedness increasing in the world, that claim remains deeply compelling to the human soul. But, even thinking about what the Beatles sang, what "love" would resolve all the world's problems? The resolution is God because *God is love—pure and holy love*.

The existence of God—His character, will, and intentions toward humanity—has been under attack for decades. The result? Many are deceived about God and don't know Him or His truth.

With this book, and the others in this *Faith to Live By* series, I ask you to reconsider all you believe and the reasons for your beliefs. If you don't, you could easily be deceived and not be aware of the deception. I realize reexamination takes courage and is quite uncomfortable. But, are you willing to suffer the *eternal* consequences for not examining what you believe?

I will provide you with reasonable arguments to prove truth is not relative, but absolute. I will also provide evidence proving the *Bible*, also referred to as *God's Word,* is unique in contrast to all other documents of religious authority. With just these two matters of truth and the Bible settled, we can then glean from the Bible, both Old and New Testaments, the truth about God. His love for you, your tremendous personal worth, your unique purpose, and how you can find meaning and true personal fulfillment in life will be unfolded.

This book is written to help you open your mind and to reconsider much of what you've been taught is true. I've written to lead you to better discover the overwhelming and *transformational* love of God—an iron-clad, secure love that allows you to realize your tremendous value and to step into your unique God-given, significant, life's purpose. Imagine the impact on the world if more people lived feeling and demonstrating God's transforming love!

There are many things that deeply grieve me. But the one thing that burdens my heart the most is the tremendous deception that prevents people from embracing all that is good—from embracing all that God wants them to enjoy—beginning and ending with His love.

I expect some will question what I mean by *God.* After all, overwhelmingly popular today is the claim that all roads lead to the same god and heaven. I addressed that deception in the first book in this series, *Examine Your Faith! Finding Truth in a World of Lies.* If you hold to the belief that all religions are equal and all lead to the same God, I ask you to intentionally reconsider. Why do you believe what you believe? What basis, what evidence do you have to support your belief? What if you are wrong? What if you are deceived? I've already proven that universally, we all want to live lives based on truth and what is good. I state again, "Unless we examine our beliefs, we can easily be deceived and not know that we are."

When I refer to *God* in the context of this book, I refer to the God of the Judeo-Christian faith, whose existence, in contrast to all other so-called gods, is distinctly unique.

My *Faith to Live By* book series is written to counter the deception rampant in society today, that all gods are equal so you can discover the same life-giving truth I've been blessed to find—the truth that will set you free and allow you to settle all the questions—all the anxieties of life—as you continue to grow in truth. Discovering and living in truth is not a one-time effort, but rather a process of discovery we must be intentional about every single day. Simply living in a world with competing claims, philosophies, and ideals can cause us to accept a matter as true when after a proper evaluation is proven to be false.

My first book, *Examine Your Faith! Finding Truth in a World of Lies*, is the foundation for the subsequent books. Book I provides arguments in support of truth, the Bible, the existence of God, and the unique life, death, and resurrection of Jesus. The book also explores the five major world religions along with New Age philosophy so you can determine for yourself if all religions are equal and if Jesus was and is who He claimed to be. The first book explores *essential faith*—or saving faith.

In the second book, *Renew Your Hope! Remedy for Personal Breakthroughs*, I seek to help people learn how to apply their faith to *experience* the many benefits God has promised to those who believe—that is those who place their faith in Jesus. Book II also explains how faith in Jesus transforms us and allows access to His power to overcome any obstacle in life. The second book explores *effective faith*—or faith that can move mountains.

This third book, *Revive Your Life! Rest for Your Anxious Heart*, explores the character of God and how His love can transform the world one person at a time. This book is about *excellent faith*, which is faith motivated by holy and perfect love.

Godly love is the motivation that produces the greatest good. My earnest prayer is for you to discover the one true God—to discover His amazing love for *you* because, though His love, you will discover tremendous joy and profound personal significance. You will be wonderfully transformed, positively influenced and take your place among those who will help change the world for the better. Indeed, all we need is love—God's love.

PART ONE

DISCOVERING LOVE

"So now faith, hope and love abide, these three; but the greatest of
these is love."

1 Corinthians 13:13

CHAPTER ONE

The Realities of Love

As you learned from the Introduction, every person desires to base their life on truth. When I ask my audiences, "Who in this room wants to live your life on the basis of a lie," no one ever raises their hand. This suggests that *universally* we prefer truth over deception.

Additionally, one of our greatest needs as human beings is to be loved. By being loved, we gain a sense of importance and significance. When another being chooses to love us, we know we are accepted, which gives us freedom to explore and grow in a loving and secure relationship.

When truth is pure, and love is unconditional, we have the optimal environment in which to become the very best we can be. In this atmosphere, we can mature and flourish and produce good from which we benefit—as do others through us.

In society, we have ample evidence of the many undesirable results that occur when truth or love are compromised or withheld. One example is the innocent children who suffer dreadful consequences in orphanages or foster homes where they are not adequately loved and may even be abused. There are many other examples in society where people suffer insufficient truth or a distorted love that adversely impacts them and thus impacts society. Inner-city children who grow up in gang- and crime-promoting communities, well-educated adults who find themselves in an abusive relationship, those who feel the impact of addiction—all are examples of situations where truth and love have been compromised. The result is human suffering.

Because you are reading this book, you must be looking for some answers to help you settle matters where you feel unfulfilled. Perhaps as I once felt, you feel anxious and frustrated with your life. Yet, you can't help but believe there must be something more—something better—available. The very fact you can't deny the sense that an answer for your unrest must exist is God at work in your life. He wants you to find the better way. He wants the best for you. In fact, He is continually at work in your life to help you discover the truth and the love you need to flourish.

We all want to live in truth, and we all need to be loved. Truth and love are two sides of the same "coin," and that coin is God. As we seek to increase our knowledge of the truth, we will increase our knowledge of God, and therefore, of love. God *is* love.

My first book in this series, *Examine Your Faith! Finding Truth in a World of Lies,* explored the five major world religions and New Age philosophy so we could conclude which religion was true. My quest was to determine which religious system was based on truth so my faith and my eternal life would not be established on faulty beliefs.

My clear and confident conclusion from that research is that *Christianity* is the one true religion based on truth and, therefore, the God of the *Christian* faith is the one true God. Christianity is the religious faith that allows people to be rightly related to God, through faith in the historical person *Jesus,* also known as *Christ* or *the Christ.* More information about the Christian faith will be provided throughout this book.

I realize you may not have read that book and you may not be ready to come to that same conclusion. With that in mind, I have provided abbreviated content from Book I in these first few chapters to help you see how I arrived at various conclusions. All the assertions I make about God are based on what we can know about the God of Christianity.

Whatever you have thought about God up to this point must be set aside. Your task, in order to find what you are searching for, is to reexamine all that you believe about religion, about God, about yourself, about your origin, and about your future. You need to be willing to reconsider all you've believed about truth and love, about good and evil, and about faith and religion. I won't try to persuade you to believe what I have come to believe. Rather, I will ask you to consider the facts as I present them to see if my conclusions are something you want to embrace or not. The choice is yours.

I hope to convince you of three things in this first chapter: 1.) God exists, 2.) All truth comes from God, and 3.) God is love.

God's Love Is Unlike Human Love

I have already taken the journey of examination upon which you are embarking. I confidently believe not only does God exist, but He is a good and loving God who is consistently at work to draw you unto Himself. God wants you to know you are made in His image by and for Him, and you have great significance and value to Him. He wants you to personally know Him and to experientially live in His love.

The kind of love that emanates from God is very different than human love. God's love is constant, unchanging, eternal, and selfless. God's love is *gift* love, whereas human love is *need* love. We need to be loved, and God is the source of the very love we need. God's love satisfies the human soul in ways that human love simply cannot. Human love has every potential of disappointing us. God's love never will.

Every person must decide if God exists or not. We will start by considering the logic and reason behind the arguments for the existence of God. Then we'll explore the character, will and intentions of God, which you will see are entirely influenced by His extravagant love for you. The hope for your life, and the discovery of your abundant worth and the disclosure of your eternal purpose, begins with considering the existence of God.

Considering the Existence and Character of God

Many believe all that exists comes from a cosmic explosion followed by the process of evolution (which I explore further in chapter three). Others believe the intricate order of creation strongly suggests intelligent design and, therefore an Intelligent Designer.

Neither evolution nor God can be scientifically proven. To prove a matter scientifically requires direct observation and measurement. The scientific method of proof requires theories be verifiable by *physical* experiment. On that basis, the existence of God, for which evidence cannot be tested, is incompatible with science. However, science is not the only method available to determine a matter. *Philosophical* proofs often provide accurate conclusions.

In the first part of his *Summa Theologica*, written in 1265–1274 AD, Thomas Aquinas, an immensely influential philosopher and theologian, provided five ways to help prove the existence of God. The *Summa* is one of the classics of the history of philosophy and one of the most influential works of Western literature. The five arguments Aquinas presented are

Motion, Efficient Causes, Possibility and Necessity, Graduation of Being, and Design.

Additionally, the argument for the existence of God is found based on the reality of Moral Law. Perhaps no one has better expressed his exploration concerning the existence and character of God through consideration of Moral Law than author, essayist, former atheist, and Christian apologist, C. S. Lewis:

> My argument against God was that the universe seemed so cruel and unjust. But how had I got this idea of just and unjust? A man does not call a line crooked unless he has some idea of a straight line. What was I comparing this universe with when I called it unjust? If the whole show was bad and senseless from A to Z, so to speak, why did I, who was supposed to be part of the show, find myself in such a violent reaction against it?
>
> … Of course, I could have given up my idea of justice by saying it was nothing but a private idea of my own. But if I did that, then my argument against God collapsed too—for the argument depended on saying the world was really unjust, not simply that it did not happen to please my fancies. Thus, in the very act of trying to prove that God did not exist—in other words, that the whole of reality was senseless—I found I was forced to assume that one part of reality—namely my idea of justice—was full of sense. If the whole universe has no meaning, we should never have found out that it has no meaning: just as, if there were no light in the universe and therefore no creatures with eyes, we should never have known it was dark. Dark would be without meaning.[1]

Many scholars have made excellent arguments to demonstrate that all of creation is the result of intelligent design, which then requires an Intelligent Designer. Intelligent design is supported by a vast body of evidence ranging from physics and cosmology to biochemistry to animal biology to systems biology to epigenetics and paleontology.

GotQuestions.org, an online ministry of dedicated volunteers, helps people in their understanding of God, Scripture, *salvation,* and other spiritual topics. Salvation is the gift God gives to those who place their faith in Jesus. Salvation will be explained more thoroughly in other areas of this book. GotQuestions.org published an article in response to the question: "What is the best evidence/argument for intelligent design?" The article stated:

> Modern scientific insight has revealed startling evidence for intelligent design from various disciplines, from biology to astronomy, from physics to cosmology.[2]

Then they provide supporting evidence for each of the four disciplines listed. Rather than summarize their supporting data here, I encourage you to visit their website for the article: https://gotquestions.org/evidence-intelligent-design.html

Bob Dutko, Christian apologist and a nationally syndicated radio talk show host, has engaged in numerous debates with atheists concerning the existence of God. I appreciate his thoroughly honest approach to the subject. When I asked Bob how he sets up the dialog, he shared:

> Technically, I cannot prove the existence of God any more than an atheist can prove that universes can create themselves. But what I can provide is the scientific law and the laws of physics that force me to conclude a belief in God is the only scientifically plausible conclusion. In the

same way, I cannot prove that George Washington was President of the United States, but I can present enough historical evidence to render illogical rejecting the belief that he was, in fact, President.

Specific to the existence of God, Bob explores the following proofs in depth. I list them here and recommend you visit his site to learn about these proofs.

1. First Law of Thermodynamics
2. Second Law of Thermodynamics
3. The Scientific Impossibility of Abiogenesis
4. The Complete Lack of Scientifically Plausible Alternatives
5. Basic Logic, Common Sense, Intellectual Reasoning
6. Mathematical Impossibilities for the Complexity of Life
7. Confirmations of Scientific Evidence within the Bible
8. Non-physical Human Characteristics
9. Existence of the Supernatural
10. Jesus, Life, Miracles, Death and Resurrection
11. Why So Many Scientists Reject Belief in God

Bob has a collection of teachings under his brand "Top Ten Proofs." I especially appreciate how he explains the topics in laymen's terms, wanting people to grasp the truths so that they can live a confident faith life. Visit Bob's website at http://www.toptenproofs.com.

Not only can we discover a wealth of logically compelling reasons to know that God exists, but we learn from this evidence He is a personal God. He is a God who desires to engage with us and to have us engage with Him. Beyond mere head knowledge of His existence, God desires we enter into a personal relationship with Him, spirit to Spirit.

One God—Many Roads?

As we've considered the existence of God, let's turn our consideration to the claim all roads lead to the same God and heaven. I addressed this considerably in *Examine Your Faith! Finding Truth in a World of Lies*. Following is a summary:

The effort to blend all religions into one, known as *syncretism*, is akin to attempting to force people to agree on fundamental matters where there can be no agreement. People who attempt to combine the tenets of different religious faiths are choosing a belief system of their own making, which is utterly unstable.

When you consider the distinctions of each of the five major world religions and New Age philosophy, you quickly realize there can be no harmonizing or blending of the different faiths without some serious compromise. Allah, the god worshiped in Islam, is believed by Muslims to be distinct from all other identified gods. The thousands of "gods" worshiped in Hinduism are diverse. The "god" of New Age philosophy is the self. In Buddhism, there is no "god" that is worshiped. The God of Judaism and Christianity is commonly believed to be the one true God among Jews and Christians. However, these differing beliefs still do not prove to us which deity is worthy of our faith.

If the distinctions made by the five major world religions are all accurate, then we must conclude the many roads lead to a god who is schizophrenic. A schizophrenic god offers no hope to anyone.

We need to test each religion to determine which makes the most logical sense to believe. Faith in something is not, as many think, blind faith devoid of any proof. Only a person who is not thinking would place his or her faith in something or someone without sufficient evidence of its worth.

The best way to discover the truth about God, in my opinion, is to compare the documents of religious authority to their oldest known manuscripts. If there are conflicts discovered by comparing the oldest known manuscript to the contemporary documents, we must scrutinize the discrepancies. If fault can be found within the "sacred writings," then perhaps there is fault within the religious belief itself.

In chapter three, I provide evidence that supports the Bible, both Old and New Testaments, as the only document of religious authority that passes the test. With the Bible uniquely verified, the religious beliefs and the God identified therein become matters worthy of our consideration.

For now, just look around you. Consider the beauty of nature—the colors of a sunset, the magnificence and power of the ocean, the order and intricacy of the universe, and the utterly fascinating complexity of the human body. Could all that exists really have simply come together over billions of years through the process of evolution?

We should consider what the apostle Paul wrote concerning man's ability to know God. "For his [God's] invisible attributes, namely, his eternal power and divine nature, have been clearly perceived, ever since the creation of the world, in the things that have been made. So they [all humanity] are without excuse [to know the one true God.] (Romans 1:20).

With at least some acknowledgment that God exists, now let's consider His character.

God is a Trinity

God is defined in the *Bible* (substantiated later in this chapter and in chapter three) as *Triune* in nature. That is, He is three Persons in one. He is God the *Father*, God the *Son*, and God the *Holy Spirit*. Each is co-equal, yet a distinct Person, with a separate role in God's interaction with all creation.

That God is a *Trinity* is exceedingly difficult if not impossible for the human mind to understand. While we are limited by our physical existence, God is not. God is spirit and infinitely more complex than we are. While the Bible clearly reveals the three Persons of God, Scripture also maintains there is only one God. The terms *tri* meaning three and *unity* meaning one, combined together form the word trinity. God is three Persons who are the same Deity but have differing roles.

The illustration of three forms of water can help us attempt to understand the Trinity. Water can be in a liquid form, a steam form or a frozen form but is still the same chemical substance. No illustration is perfect, but as you seek to grow in your knowledge of God, you'll come to embrace the Trinity and how God interacts with us as Father, as Son or Savior, and as Holy Spirit.

God is Love

The phrase *God is love* explicitly appears in the Bible only twice. Both times the three-word phrase appears as penned by the apostle John in 1 John 4:8 and 4:16. To truly comprehend what the statement means is not only key to understanding God but is essential to becoming willing to place your faith in God. Those who misunderstand the character of God will not be attracted to Him. Being rightly convinced that God is love allows us to willingly enter into a *holy*, loving relationship with Him with access to all the blessings and benefits He offers in this life and in eternal life. A holy relationship with God is *sacred* and is characterized by deeply reverent dedication and unadulterated devotion.

If your view of God is that He is harsh, judgmental, and unloving, keeping your distance would make sense. Unfortunately, that's how many people see God, and this incorrect understanding prevents many people from experiencing all the tremendous benefits of being rightly related to God.

The love God offers is unlike the love we humans offer. God's love is pure, holy, and constantly reliable. The love God offers is unconditional, which means there is nothing you can do to earn more of God's love, and there's nothing you can do to diminish God's love. God's love is bestowed upon you beyond time itself. God's love reaches into the deep recesses of eternity past and is stretched all the way forward into eternity future. The Bible states in Ephesians 1:4-6 "even as he chose us *in him* before the foundation of the world, that we should be holy and blameless before him. In love, he predestined us for adoption as sons through *Jesus Christ,* according to the purpose of his will, to the praise of his glorious grace, with which he has blessed us in the *Beloved*" (emphasis added).

The term *in him* means the Father knows those who will believe in and receive Jesus as their personal Savior. Those who choose to believe in God are predestined to be adopted into God's family through faith in Jesus (the Beloved in this verse). We are united to God, who is love, when we have repented of our sins and have accepted Jesus Christ as our Lord and Savior. His Holy Spirit is then given to us as the guarantor of our adoption. God's love for you existed before you were ever conceived and will continue for all eternity.

God the Son is known primarily as Jesus, Christ, Jesus Christ, or Jesus the Christ.

The word *Christ* comes from the Greek word *Christianos,* meaning "follower of Christ," and also comes from *Christos,* meaning "anointed one" with an adjectival ending borrowed from Latin to denote adhering to, or even belonging to. So, a *Christian* is one who follows Christ. The term *believer* is also often used when referring to a Christian. Jesus is also referred to as the Son of God and the Son of Man. Much more about the historical person, Jesus, will be discussed in chapter four. As you continue reading, you will come to clearly see how God personally demonstrated His love for you through Jesus.

While the fact God's love precedes our existence is absolutely true, if we want to enter into His love *fully*, we need to respond to the *terms* of the offer. While God's love is unconditional, most of His promises aren't. If we want to enjoy the benefits of His stated promises, we need to position our self as He instructs, then we can enjoy the full benefit of the particular promise.

Please don't confuse God's terms for receiving a promise with His unconditional love. Most often, human love is conditional, meaning we love others so long as certain conditions are satisfied. What conditions we each want to be satisfied to continue to extend our love vary from person to person. People claim to "fall out of love" on the basis of some condition that no longer is satisfied. Not so with God. His love is unconditional.

However, many of His promises require specific action on our part to position ourselves to receive the promise. As an example, if we want to fully enjoy God's love we need to *place our faith in Jesus*. Faith in Jesus positions us in a right standing or *relationship* with God. From that point, we are in a position to satisfy specific terms to receive specific promises—not a difficult or exasperating journey. God is very clear—if you do this, I will do that. God wants His people to work in partnership with Him to receive His good and perfect gifts or promises. Knowing God is not about religion, but is entirely about the relationship.

The wisdom and beauty in God's manner of fulfilling promises bring us along in the process of receiving a greater revelation of truth, love, and holiness. And God is actively at work within us to help us do His good will because He wants us to have an overflowing abundance of His gifts and promises.

Discovering Truth

Just as God's existence and character have been woefully misunderstood for centuries, so has truth itself been misunderstood. Truth is the foundation each of us wants for our life, so let's examine truth next.

In the first book of this *Faith to Live By* series, I explored the topic of truth vs. *relativism* in reasonable detail. Here is a short consideration.

Relativism is the view that truth is personal—that what is true for me is my truth and what is true for you is your truth, even if the two are at odds.

Cultural relativism is the view that all beliefs, customs, and ethics are relative to the individual within their own social and cultural context. What is considered "right" and "wrong" are culture-specific. No universal standard of morality exists, and no one has the right to judge another society's customs. Since truth is not objective, there can be no objective standard which applies to all cultures. *Ethical relativism,* closely related to cultural relativism, views truth as variable and not absolute. What constitutes right and wrong is determined solely by the individual or society.

Relativism is the reason for the increasing acceptance of differing cultural expressions even when the expression results in harm.

> In January 2002, when President Bush referred to terrorist nations as an "axis of evil," the cultural relativists were mortified. That any society would call another society "evil" is anathema to the relativist. The current movement to "understand" radical Islam "rather than to fight it" is a sign that relativism is making gains. The cultural relativist believes Westerners should not impose their ideas on the Islamic world, including the idea that the suicide bombing of civilians is evil. Islamic belief in the necessity of jihad is

just as valid as any belief in Western civilization, the relativists assert, and America is as much to blame for the attacks of 9/11 as are the terrorists.[3]

Unfortunately, many people have accepted the concept of celebrating diversity to the extreme. Even though relativism claims there is no universal standard for truth or morals, in reality, there is. For most of the world, lying, cheating, stealing, slavery, rape, and murder, for example, are wrong and are not to be tolerated to protect both the common good of society and of individuals. The effects of relativism are chaos and destruction, whereas the effects of absolute truth are order and protection.

Those who believe truth is relative might say, "There is no such thing as absolute truth." Well, that statement in itself *is* an absolute statement.

Any matter can be tested to determine if it is true by using all three of the following proof tests:

1. Truth always lines up with reality.
2. Only one thing can be true; all opposing matters are false.
3. The truth is universal.

Simply claiming a matter to be true, does not make it so. The person making a claim has the responsibility to prove the claim. Countless numbers of people today are deceived, and, true to the nature of deception, they don't know it. While universally we all want to live our lives on the basis of truth, unless we intentionally make an effort to examine what we believe, we could easily base our life on a lie. When lies and deception are the foundations of our beliefs, we are certain to suffer. When truth is our life's foundation, we are in a position to enjoy the best life offers.

As instructed in the Bible, the Christian religion is to value people from all cultures recognizing and even celebrating the beauty in cultural distinctions. However, harmful practices of any people group are not to be tolerated. All the standards and morals in the Bible are established for our individual good and the good of societies.

With that in mind, let's next consider the authority of the Bible, which is not accepted by *liberal theology,* (liberal theology will be explored in chapter two).

The Test of Scriptures

There are generations of people who think the Bible (also referred to as *The Scriptures or Scripture*) is no different from any other so-called document of religious authority. They believe the Bible is to be equally respected along with the Koran, the Tripitaka, the writings of Buddha, and so on. And there are those who believe the Bible is nothing more than a product of various religious cultures and peoples who recorded their experiences with God *as they imagined Him to be.* Many conclude the Bible is not at all relevant for today. For this reason, in *Examine Your Faith! Finding Truth in a World of Lies,* I provided verifiable information with historical, archeological, and extra-biblical evidence, sufficiently proving the Bible to be *divinely inspired* and, therefore, unique in contrast to all other so-called documents of religious authority. Next, I offer just a cursory overview from *Examine Your Faith! Finding Truth in a World of Lies.*

One of the most sensational archeological discoveries of our age is the discovery of the Dead Sea Scrolls. These scrolls and fragments of scrolls, also called manuscripts, written in Hebrew, Aramaic, and Greek, provide the oldest manuscript of the Old Testament, predating the previously oldest known manuscripts by over *1000 years.* This discovery pushes the date of the oldest known manuscripts of the Bible to the second century BC.

The Dead Sea Scrolls provide objective, verifiable evidence that proves the Bible we have today is substantively unchanged as compared to the scrolls. If the Bible has remained unchanged for more than two-thousand years, then we can easily believe the Scriptures have remained unchanged since originally penned.

Consider too, the sixty-six books of the Old and New Testaments that comprise the Protestant Bible were penned by forty different authors over a span of approximately fifteen hundred years, in three different languages and covering hundreds of subjects. Yet, amazingly, with such a vast compilation and without any personal collaboration, there is no conflict of information. From the Old Testament through the New Testament there is one constant theme—God's redemption of mankind.

A genuine, open-minded approach to learning about the Bible reveals the Scriptures could not be written by men without being divinely inspired. How else can you justify the veracity? The Bible is the divine revelation of God, penned by men as a means for God to communicate and connect with humanity. This divinely inspired document reveals the truth about God and His transforming love. The Bible also reveals His grand plan to redeem the entire world—ridding the world of sickness, death, destruction, and evil.

If we accept the huge amount of historical, archeological, scientific, and other evidence that demonstrates the reliability of the Bible, both Old and New Testaments, then we can confidently study these Scriptures to learn about God, His character, will, and intentions toward humanity.

God's gift of His written Word is another demonstration of His love for us. We have documentation of His intervention in humanity that reveals His faithful, loving character, as well as His retribution when we disobey His will. God's will for us is always with our best interest in mind. Just as earthly parents punish their children for their own good, God does the same with us. We have His promises recorded, to pore over, to reassure us, and to stand on to experience His goodness. We can grow in our knowledge of God and His love by studying His Word, the Holy Bible.

God's Love is Our Joy

Richard L. Strauss, in his article *God is Love*, published in the "Joy of Knowing God" series, wrote:

> To know Him [God] is to find release from the crippling effects of feeling unloved. Love is one of the warmest words in the English language, and that God is love is one of the most sublime, uplifting and reassuring truths known to mankind. Love is His nature. It is not merely a friendly attitude He projects. It is the essence of His being. He is always going to act toward us in love because He cannot do otherwise. Love is His way. No one attribute of God is any more important than any other, and all His attributes are expressed in conjunction with each other. Yet some believe that love may be the most powerful motivating force in all of God's being. It deeply affects everything else God is and all that He does. Knowing God's love could well be the believer's key to a well-balanced, satisfying life of peace, productivity, and power.[4]

To ever exhaust the subject of God's love would be impossible for us. Yet, our best interest is served by ever learning more and more. Seven characteristics of God's love are:

1. God's Love is Self-Giving—The opposite of love is not hate; it's selfishness. Genuine love involves action that provides

expression in giving oneself for the benefit of another. Love, therefore, always demands at least one object. If love demands at least one object, then how did He express love before He created angels or humanity? This question takes us back to the reality that God is a Trinity. Love was demonstrated between the Persons of the Trinity from eternity past and on into eternity future. God is complete and sufficient in Himself. He does not need anything beyond Himself to express His nature. However, God chose to create angels and humanity to have even more opportunity to express Himself. From His love, God communes with us, gives of Himself to us, and bestows His very best on us for our benefit and blessing.

2. God's Love is Sacrificial—God's love motivates Him to give, even when what He gives costs Him dearly. There is no greater example of this than in the sacrifice of God the Son in the person of Jesus. John 3:16 makes this abundantly clear: "For God so loved the world, that he gave his only Son, that whoever believes in him should not perish but have eternal life." God personally took on human form, willingly gave up His rightful place in heaven, for a time to suffer and die in our place, to pay the awful debt of sin that we owe but could not pay, and then rose again conquering sin and death forever. God proved His love conclusively and irrefutably through the sacrifice and resurrection of God the Son.

3. God's Love is Unconditional—While we were yet sinners, and at complete enmity with God, He loved us. God always loves us even when we don't respond to His love. "God so loved the world ..." does not mean the world as a group. Rather, His love is extended individual by individual. God's love for us

is what establishes our worth. The fact God Himself has chosen to love us is evidence enough that we are highly significant just as we are. But, oh, how much more world-impacting are we when we cooperate with God's plan for our life.

4. God's Love is Eternal—God Himself is infinite and, therefore, so is His love. The apostle Paul, attempting to explain this truth, wrote that God's love is a love that surpasses knowledge (Ephesians 3:19) meaning it's far greater than our limited minds can comprehend. Paul referred to the breadth, length, depth, and height of God's love to demonstrate His love is immeasurable.

5. God's Love is Holy—Since God Himself is holy, so is anything that emanates from Him. We must note that God's love being holy encourages holiness in the objects of His love. When we fall outside the parameters of His will, His love motivates Him to bring us back. Therefore, even His discipline of those He loves is a demonstration of His love.

6. God's Love is Comforting—In God's love, we are secure, safe, and nurtured. Through faith in Jesus, we belong to God. And if we belong to Him, we are His responsibility. That's not to imply we have no part in tending to our own needs. Rather, we need not fear anything in life when we are submitted to God's love and His ways.

7. God's Love is Life-Changing—I've heard the saying, "Hurting people hurt people," and I know from experience this is true. But those who discover God's love for them are transformed from the pain of this world, and they experience the

transforming power of God's love, allowing them to find healing, wholeness, and purpose that is otherwise non-existent.

In the next chapter, we'll explore how humanity has become deceived about a proper understanding of God and His love.

CHAPTER TWO

The Condition of our Culture

An inordinate number of people are deceived. How are people deceived? By simply accepting a matter to be true without verifying the facts. Could you be deceived? I believe anyone who does not regularly examine what they believe and why they believe it, could easily be deceived.

The first book in this *Faith to Live By* series was inspired when I read an article by *ABC News* about Americans being flexible about religious beliefs. The article revealed how a growing number of Americans are choosing different tenets of various religious faiths to make a "religion" of their own preference.[1] This makes the individual "god" and the supreme authority over his or her life, while utterly disregarding *irrefutable truth*—a concept explained later in this chapter. Our culture has become so confounded, no wonder people are restless.

When many people look to leadership, government, financial experts, and the like to solve the ills of society, the deception is fueled. The solution is not available in any world system. In fact, a sound argument can be made the increasing corruption of world-systems has brought us to the condition we're in. In my lifetime, I have never seen a greater divide between people.

The ability to have rational conversations to quell differences is rare. More often, people resort to personal attacks, both verbal and physical. We are divided on nearly every level and "create camps" to fortify the divisions in our philosophies. I firmly believe the only solution is to increase the proper knowledge of God.

Philosopher Dr. Alice von Hildebrand advised the following:

> Now let us abolish the terms "conservative" or "liberal," the terms "left" and "right" which are secularistic. I suggest that we say from now on "those who have kept the sense of the supernatural and those who have lost it." That is the great divide, that is the essence.[2]

Dr. von Hildebrand's suggestion, in the context of her essay, refers to recognizing the supernatural reality of God and the personal and transforming relationship anyone who desires, can have with Him. She recognizes people not on the basis of their choice in politics, which is a world system. Rather, she suggests we recognize people based on their embrace or rejection of God.

Division of Two Worlds

Today in our world, we have a vast number of people who adhere to the *secular* point of view. That is, most people operate their lives on the basis there is no need for religion. Secularists claim there is no spiritual basis for life—no deity. This is a natural conclusion from the belief all that exists was created by an explosion (the *Big Bang Theory of Evolution*) and everything in creation today evolved from that great cosmic event. If this is true, then it makes complete sense people would conclude there is no significant purpose to life. Their philosophy is "We come from nothing, and our end is nothing, so how we live our life in between is entirely up to us." At the heart of this mindset is the desire to live as they please without being subject to any greater authority than themselves. The *theory* of evolution that has been *taught as fact* is but one major reason people feel hopeless and lacking in purpose.

I firmly believe, however, that people who hold to *secular humanism*, (belief that humanity is capable of morality and self-fulfillment without belief in God) experience a relentless, nagging sense something is missing.

The Search for More

Perhaps there has been no generation of people who have been so adversely impacted by liberalism and social engineering than the *millennial generation* (those born 1981-1996). The Pew Research Center published a report entitled "How Millennials Today Compare with their Grandparents 50 Years Ago." In summary of the Millennials the report states:

> The past five decades—spanning from the time when the *Silent generation* (today, mostly in their 70s and 80s) was entering adulthood, to the adulthood of today's Millennials—have seen large shifts in U.S. society and culture. It has been a period during which Americans, especially Millennials, have become more detached from major institutions like political parties, religion, the military, and marriage. At the same time, the racial and ethnic makeup of the country has changed, college attainment has spiked, and women have greatly increased their participation in the nation's workforce and their representation on college campuses.[3]

Millennials came of adult age during very tough times. In 2014, the millennial generation age range was 18-33. Millennials entered the workforce during the nation's Great Recession. Other generations certainly faced tough employment markets as they entered adulthood, such as the *boomers* (those born 1946-1964) did during the 1981-1982 recession. However, the economic and labor markets have been very slow in recovery following the deepest recession in decades. Many millennials are greatly discouraged with some suffering depression and hopelessness.

I personally understand the toll that under- and unemployment takes as my husband and I suffered for four years when our children were less than five years old. During those years, we lost virtually everything material, our health suffered as did our marriage, and we racked up a considerable debt. Even though the cause of our situation was beyond our control, the sense of failure we experienced was immense. But for millennials, there is an underlying pressure driving them to out-perform their parents, which adds to the angst they endure.

Melanie Curtin, a contributing writer for *Inc. Magazine*, polled over three-hundred millennials regarding the pressure to succeed and wrote her article "Why Millennials Should Stop Trying to Be Successful ... Immediately." She reports:

> I got responses like: "I spent the past weekend in San Francisco, [the] epicenter of the Millennial overachiever. I was supposed to be on vacation. Instead, I developed an inordinate amount of stress over the fact that I have yet to start and go public with my own company."
>
> It turns out Millennials do feel more pressure. 67 percent of them said they felt "extreme" pressure to succeed, compared to 40 percent of *Gen Xers* [those born 1965-1980] and 23 percent of Boomers. There was a

marked difference in the open-ended responses of Millennials, too—an overall mood of anxiety and self-reproach. The majority felt ... they hadn't done enough yet, and time was running out.

According to recent research from the University of Pittsburgh School of Medicine, the more time young adults spend on social media, the more likely they are to be depressed. In fact, study participants who checked social media the most frequently throughout the week were 2.7x more likely to experience depression.

Millennials came of age during the era of social media, and a large number of survey respondents pointed out the fact that social media was a trigger—seeing how well everyone else seemed to be doing often had them feel worse, and like they had to do more to catch up.[4]

Melanie explained for the millennials, it's not a matter of seeking recognition. Instead, it's a sense of shame—feeling that they haven't done enough with their life by age twenty-five.

In my observations, with the reality that millennials are a product of public education in the era when America largely reflected the secular humanistic worldview and the belief that all that exists came from a cosmic explosion, they have no awareness of anything greater than themselves. This naturally creates additional pressure for them to be the world's much-needed change agents.

The problems millennials suffer are not limited to America. Just over a year ago, I interviewed Louis and Janey DeMeo for a television program. Louis had been pastoring for over forty years at that time. He and Janey were missionaries, church planters, and Bible teachers in France for twenty-two years. They taught at the Theological Institute they founded in Nîmes, France. They stated the millennials in France have an even more difficult time finding employment than those in America and that the depression and suicide rate among them is the one of the highest in the world. France ranks #47 of 170 countries in suicides, with an overall suicide rate of 12.3 per 100,000 people in 2012—higher than Germany or the United Kingdom.[5]

I admire the deep-seated desire to make a positive difference in this world for the good of society. Millennials often talk about wanting to be part of a revolution. However, it's my hope that my life-work will help them find the truth and the freedom truth brings. The weight of the world is not on their shoulders. God is continually offering a way for each of us to make a difference in this world for the better—the very God the millennials know precious little about.

Brene Brown speaks beautifully about the basic human desire of connecting to someone greater than ourselves. Brene is an American scholar, author, and public speaker, who is currently a research professor at the University of Houston Graduate College of Social Work. In a 2010 Ted Talk, she shared:

> I believe that we long to be connected to each other, to know and be known. There is something more for me, however. I also believe that we are hard-wired to seek connection to the Divine and that deep within every one of us is the desire to be in relationship with something or someone greater than our human potential, something or someone bigger than ourselves.
>
> Certainly, this would explain why people go to church or to synagogue or practice meditation in Sangha gatherings; but I think our desire is demonstrated in other ways as

well. I think this is also the reason we make art, write poetry, and seek beauty in creation. We want to be in relationship with other humans, with animals, with nature; but I also think we are in search of that relationship with the Divine.[6]

Stop for a moment and ponder what Lynne Hinton wrote—very specifically as her words apply to you. Are you satisfied with life? Do you have deep satisfaction and comfort in your relationships with other people? Do you have faith in something bigger than yourself? If not, or if you are not fully convinced there is anything greater than yourself, *would you like*, in your heart of hearts, there to be a loving Deity who is deeply concerned with every aspect of your life?

Of the many different religious faiths, only the God of the Judeo-Christian faith can be described as a loving Deity, who is deeply concerned with every aspect of your life. There is far more we can explore regarding getting to know God, all of which is exceedingly appealing to the *unbiased* human soul. If more people rightly knew *about* God, they would embrace Him without hesitation. Unfortunately, the enemy of God—the *devil* or *Satan*—has prevented many from knowing the truth about God by twisting the truth and causing great numbers of people to base their life on lies.

I lived the first nearly thirty years of my life deceived and unaware of the deception. Not until I encountered a crisis that challenged everything I'd ever believed did I realize my life was based on lies. My religious faith and worldview were not based on reliable truth. As a result, the crisis I suffered obliterated my beliefs leaving me with no clear direction to navigate myself out of the devastation. This blindsiding crisis, however, caused me to finally realize the faulty foundation of my life. With that much knowledge, I was then able to start to rebuild my life's foundation. You don't have to suffer a devastating crisis to ensure your life is based on truth. Instead, it's my hope you will find the confident hope and absolute certainty you need within the pages of this book.

Humanism's Impact on Culture

In my lifetime in America, I have seen a major cultural shift from most people believing in the existence of God, and having respect for and acceptance of the Bible with its instructions for life to the nearly complete rejection of all these truths and values.

How has our world become so radically changed? The changes started with deception and continue with deception. There has certainly been a mass ebb and flow of societal norms and cultures since the beginning of time. But I trace our current cultural condition to the extended period known as *the Enlightenment.* Beginning with the period known as the *French Enlightenment* (in the eighteenth century) with the emphasis on the primacy of human reason, the truth about God, about humanity, and about *truth itself* became corrupted. By emphasizing reason and logic from the human perspective, devoid of any "God" perspective, we have skewed a right understanding of truth, and as a result, vast numbers of people are living with deceptions. While the period of Enlightenment impacted many aspects of our culture, perhaps none has been more severely impacted than religious faith.

The French period of Enlightenment gave birth to the German period, which directly impacted religious faith—specifically what became known as *Protestant Liberalism.* Protestant Liberalism is defined as follows:

> Theological liberalism, sometimes known as *Protestant Liberalism,* is a theological movement rooted in the early 19th century German Enlightenment, notably in the

philosophy of Immanuel Kant and the religious views of Friedrich Schleiermacher. It is an attempt to incorporate modern thinking and developments, especially in the sciences, into the Christian faith. Liberalism tends to emphasize ethics over doctrine and experience over Scriptural authority. While essentially a 19th-century movement, theological liberalism came to dominate the American mainline churches in the early 20th century. Liberal Christian scholars embraced and encouraged the higher biblical criticism of modern biblical scholarship [encouraged people to reject the authority of the Bible].

Protestant liberal thought in its most traditional incarnations emphasized the universal Fatherhood of God, the brotherhood of man, the infinite value of the human soul, the example of Jesus, and the establishment of the moral-ethical Kingdom of God on Earth. It has often been relativistic, pluralistic, and non-doctrinal.

Liberalism birthed other movements with varying emphases. Among these movements have been the Social Gospel, Liberation Theology, Process Theology, Theological Feminism, and the Jesus Seminar. One product of these movements is the heretical Myth of Christian Origins which denies the divinity of Christ and the authority of Scripture.[7]

How the Church Became Irrelevant

Liberal Christian teaching is considered by most to be not Christian at all. Rather, human reasoning is emphasized and regarded as the final authority. Science is considered as all-knowing and the Bible as an ancient, fable-laden document that is no longer relevant. "Liberalism's disregard for the church's long-standing claim that Scripture is divinely inspired and authoritative has left its adherents with authority residing only in their own minds, and with understandings of what is acceptable that are mere echoes of secular values."[8]

> Protestant Liberalism has significant influence. Its underlying theological position is held by most of the leadership and professors in the theological seminaries of several mainline denominations in the United States (the Episcopal Church, the Evangelical Lutheran Church in America, the United Methodist Church, the American Baptist Convention, the Presbyterian Church-USA, and the United Church of Christ), though all these denominations still have some conservative evangelical congregations, teachers and people within them as well. In addition, Protestant Liberalism is the most common viewpoint in campus ministry offices in secular universities, and also among the professors who teach the Bible in religion departments of those universities. (Campus para-church ministries, however, tend to be more in line with evangelical Protestantism.)[9]

When human reason replaces divine revelation, when cultural relativism replaces absolute truth, and when human optimism replaces divine salvation, what we have is humanity seeking to determine what is right and what is wrong, and seeking to claim what is truth and what is error. These ideas are nothing new, although far more rampant in our postmodern culture than any other time in history. And this reality is preventing countless numbers of people from discovering the truth about God—who personifies the very love we need to discover our true value and life's purpose.

Man's Innate Desire for God

There is an often used quote ascribed to Blaise Pascal: "There is a God-shaped vacuum in the heart of every person, and it can never be filled by any created thing. It can only be filled by God, made known through Jesus Christ." (The person *Jesus Christ* is explained in chapters one and four.) This quote is a condensed version of Pascal's actual statement:

> What else does this craving, and this helplessness, proclaim but that there was once in man a true happiness, of which all that now remains is the empty print and trace?
>
> This he tries in vain to fill with everything around him, seeking in things that are not there the help he cannot find in those that are, though none can help, since this infinite abyss can be filled only with an infinite and immutable object; in other words by God Himself.[10]

Blaise Pascal, born 1623, was a French mathematician, physicist, and religious philosopher, who along with Pierre de Fermat, laid the foundation for the modern theory of probabilities. In the 1650s, *Les Provinciales* was published in a theological work that turned out to be a groundbreaking series of letters emphasizing *original sin, human depravity*, the necessity of *divine grace*, and *predestination*. Pascal is also widely known for his body of notes posthumously released as the *Pensées*, which defended his Christian faith. Pascal died in Paris on August 19, 1662.

The concept that humanity was created by God with a desire to personally know Him is supported throughout the entire Bible.

The Innate Desire to Belong

Wanting to be part of something—the need to belong—is born out in *Maslow's Hierarchy of Needs,* a theory in *psychology* proposed by Abraham Maslow in his 1943 paper, "A Theory of Human Motivation" in *Psychological Review.* Maslow's theory is comprised of a five-tier model of human needs, often depicted as hierarchical levels in the shape of a pyramid. Maslow's study was that of learning what motivates people. His theories parallel many other theories of human-development psychology. Moving from the base of the pyramid to the top, the terms for the discoveries Maslow observed are, "physiological," "safety," "belongingness and love," "esteem," and "self-actualization."[11]

The top three tiers are of special significance for this book—belongingness love, esteem, and self-actualization. If Maslow's theory is correct, then we all desire to belong and be loved, to be esteemed, and to enjoy the realization or fulfillment of our talents and potentialities (self-actualization). I don't see these desires being satisfied in even the slightest degree with the belief that all creation has come from a cosmic event followed by evolution and the survival of the fittest. If all of creation, including humanity, is the result of a random explosion, then there is no basis for virtues such as heroism, selflessness, human kindness, or morality of any kind—there is no origin for any expression of love.

Contributors to Wikipedia provide additional insight:

> Belongingness is the human emotional need to be an accepted member of a group. Whether it is family, friends, co-workers, a religion, or something else, people tend to

have an 'inherent' desire to belong and be an important part of something greater than themselves. This implies a relationship that is greater than simple acquaintance or familiarity. The need to belong is the need to give, and receive attention to, and from, others.

Belonging is a strong and inevitable feeling that exists in human nature. To belong or not to belong can occur due to choices of one's self, or the choices of others. Not everyone has the same life and interests, hence not everyone belongs to the same thing or person. Without belonging, one cannot identify themselves as clearly, thus having difficulties communicating with and relating to their surroundings.

Roy Baumeister and Mark Leary argue that belongingness is such a fundamental human motivation that we feel severe consequences of not belonging. If it wasn't so fundamental, then lack of belonging wouldn't have such dire consequences on us. This desire is so universal that the need to belong is found across all cultures and different types of people.[12]

Interpreting Our Longings

Why would we desire to belong, unless we were created to function in community? Why would any of us feel unloved, unless we were created to experience love? How can anyone of us feel a sense of insignificance, unless we were created with a desire to be significant? The fact we can be unsettled and anxious with a desire for meaning and purpose in life is evidence our existence is not the result of a random beginning, but rather an intentional beginning.

The desire to find God and to belong and be loved are, in my considered opinion, two more attestations to the fact that humanity was intentionally created, and is not a result of some cosmic explosion.

I think of the strong allure of gang membership for many inner-city kids. They are simply seeking to have some basic needs met that are otherwise not being satisfied. I spoke before the City Council once on behalf of my church. We had applied for a permit to build a new sanctuary and were being met with opposition. Having come from a law enforcement family, I sought to get input from a former Chief of Police, who is like an uncle to me. I was looking for statistics and such to substantiate my argument. But, by quoting this former Police Chief to the City Council, I made my point. He said, "As a retired law enforcement officer who has seen a lot of senseless violence, I would personally encourage not only the expansion of this church but of all churches. Because if the church doesn't get stray people first, the police surely will."

Could it be that these desires—to belong, to be loved and to be significant—are driving forces that cause people to do many things that result in harm? For example, sexual deviancy, drug addictions, pornography, prostitution, et al. How many people have fallen into these horrendous realities out of a deep sense of needing their innate desires to be loved and to belong fulfilled?

If you are one who has dabbled in lifestyles or behaviors that have left you still feeling unfulfilled or have made your life worse, you still have another choice. You still have hope. My belief is the desires to belong, to be loved and to be significant are evidence that we are created by God in His image for His created purpose. And unless we are functioning according to our created purpose, we have no hope of finding true, personal fulfillment.

Social Movements and Culture Shifts

I've seen many social and political movements in my lifetime. I've also seen many religious movements that seem to be a response to the social and cultural unrest. When I was young during the early 1960s and 1970s, there was the counter-culture Hippie movement; the anti-discrimination movement led by Dr. Martin Luther King, Jr.; and the Jesus movement. Clearly, for all these to arise around the same time, there had to have been a considerable amount of pent-up unrest and dissatisfaction with life on many levels. I think that's like what we see now in America.

With the Presidential election of November 2016, we saw a tremendous shift from what the media, at least, expected. While the shift has political implications, we are also seeing trending religious implications. There is a great divide in America and heightened levels of anxiety and unrest for a variety of reasons.

However, within all this anxiety and unrest, I sense tremendous positive excitement. When people are satisfied or complacent, there is no desire for change. Only when things become sufficiently uncomfortable are people willing to act to bring change. Behind the response of the people today, we have an increasing awareness of God initiating His intervention in the lives of His people. What we are seeing is not a movement initiated by humanity, but an utterly planned strategic intervention of God to bring about much-needed reform.

I believe the release of this book will coordinate with God's plans. This excites me for you, dear reader. Because I believe God is orchestrating situations and circumstances in every area of society—business, government, media, arts/entertainment, education, the family, and religion.

Not only in America, but in many other countries and cultures, there is a shifting taking place. I believe God is calling forth people from every nation, to find their rightful place in relationship with Him. As I wrote in the Introduction, "Imagine the impact on the world if more people lived in God's transforming love!"

I believe we are in one of the greatest seasons the world has ever known and we should be excited to be alive now. If greater numbers of people discover the truth about God, we will see droves of people running into God's arms of love. However, we must be wise. There is an enemy of God who works overtime to try to prevent you and me from entering into God's plan and promises. Just as any intelligence agency does, we must know our enemy. The next chapter is intended to better equip you to know our enemy and to be able to take hold of the victory that is already ours through Christ.

CHAPTER THREE

The Distortion of Truth

In our culture, God has been made to be whatever a person wants it to be in an effort to purge anything deemed uncomfortable or undesirable. This is entirely consistent with what I wrote in *Examine Your Faith! Finding Truth in a World of Lies* concerning people creating "religious beliefs" based on their own personal preferences.

As stated in the previous chapter, whole groups of people have rejected the church and the Bible either in its entirety or selectively, which is to reject the Word or "Life Manual" from the very God who created us and has repeatedly demonstrated His love for us.

Our culture's claim to be enlightened and governed by rational thought is inspired by deception. In reality, the culture is governed by subjective personal feelings. Even our language has been altered. Rarely do you hear a person state, "I think." More often we hear, "I feel."

The reason for this is simple. Our desire is to be "god" of our own life, deciding what is true and false—what is right and wrong. When a person claims, "I feel," there is no ability for anyone else to challenge them. We cannot challenge what a person *feels*. However, when a person claims, "I think," we can challenge them with the question, "On what basis or authority do you think as you do?" Then, the onus is on the person to substantiate their claim under the scrutiny of objective logic and reason.

Two of my highly esteemed mentors, C. S. Lewis and J. I. Packard, both bestselling authors and theologians, expressed how difficult the human effort of comprehending the claim that *God is love* actually is. Packard wrote, "St. John's twice-repeated statement, "God is love" is one of the most tremendous utterances in the Bible—and also one of the most misunderstood. False ideas have grown up round it like a hedge of thorns, hiding its real meaning from view, and it is no small task cutting through this *tangle of mental undergrowth"* [emphasis added].[1]

When our objective is to understand the truth, we need to approach the subject from the Truth-giver's perspective. In our flawed, natural human condition (explained later in this chapter), we want to be the one who defines truth—the one who determines what truth or good is, and what is false or bad. This reality is a large reason for the tangle of mental undergrowth we need to cut through.

Misunderstanding the Love of God

D. A. Carson, research professor of New Testament at Trinity Evangelical Divinity School and author of *The Difficult Doctrine of the Love of God*, explains there are at least five reasons why the doctrine of God's love is difficult. Those reasons are condensed here:

> 1) If people believe in God at all today, the overwhelming majority hold that this God—however he, she, or it may be understood—is a loving being…[T]his widely disseminated belief in the love of God is set with increasing frequency in some matrix other than biblical theology.

2) [W]e live in a culture in which many other and complementary truths about God are widely *dis*believed. I do not think that what the Bible says about the love of God can long survive at the forefront of our thinking if it is abstracted from the sovereignty of God, the holiness of God, the wrath of God, the providence of God, or the personhood of God—to mention only a few nonnegotiable elements of basic Christianity. The result, of course, is that the love of God in our culture has been purged of anything the culture finds uncomfortable. The love of God has been sanitized, democratized, and above all, sentimentalized. Today most people seem to have little difficulty believing in the love of God; they have far more difficulty believing in the justice of God, the wrath of God, and the non-contradictory truthfulness of an omniscient [all-knowing] God.

3) Because of remarkable shifts in the West's *epistemology* [the theory of knowledge/investigating justified belief from opinion], more and more people believe that the only heresy left is the view that there is no such thing as heresy. They hold that all religions are fundamentally the same and that therefore, it is not only rude but profoundly ignorant and old-fashioned to try to win someone to your beliefs since implicitly that is announcing that theirs is inferior.

4) In the cultural rush toward a sentimentalized, sometimes even non-theistic vision of the love of God, we *Christians* have ...been swept along [forgetting] that within *Christian confessionalism* [belief in the importance of full and unambiguous assent to the whole of Christian teaching],

the doctrine of the love of God poses its difficulties. Precisely how does one integrate what the Bible says about the love of God with what the Bible says about God's sovereignty, extending as it does even over the domain of evil? What does love mean in a Being whom at least some texts treat as impassible? How is God's love tied to justice? 5) [T]he doctrine of the love of God is sometimes portrayed within Christian circles as much easier and more obvious than it really is, and this is achieved by overlooking some of the distinctions the Bible itself introduces when it depicts the love of God.[2]

Let me comment on the five points D. A. Carson has made point by point.

1) Many desire God to be loving so *they* may benefit. They think God's love motivates Him to indulge their every desire, provide for them in abundance, and be available at their beck and call. This is a perversion of what Scriptures say about God and His love. This point of view makes the individual the object of God's worship, instead of the other way around.

2) We must understand God is love, but that is not all He is. His love motivates everything He does. What is at stake here is having our own idea of what love is. How many times have you heard a person say, "A loving God would never _______"? Such a statement is saying that "I have my own idea of what love is and anything outside that idea is not acceptable." This is a subtle form of idolatry that many people, even professing Christians, fall prey to.

3) There's a rapidly growing trend in America to consider those who believe in God of the Bible as utter buffoons. In this culture of

tolerance, everything is tolerated except the tenets of the Christian faith. The sad truth is this cultural influence has adversely impacted the Christian's willingness to witness effectively, leaving even more people deceived.

4)   The doctrine of God's love is difficult. Proverbs 25:2 states: "It is the glory of God to conceal things, but the glory of kings is to search things out." Searching to learn more about God is certain to lead you to discover the answers to all your life questions and find the personal fulfillment you desire. Unfortunately, most people think they are enlightened and already have the truth, so they don't bother to consider they might be wrong.

5)   The love of God must never be reduced to and understood from the human perspective. Rather, we need to understand the love of God from the Divine perspective. Scriptures challenge us to love our neighbor and even our enemies with Godly love. The only way we can do that is if we have entered God's love and allow His love to flow from us. Then we will see a better world emerge.

In short, the most energetic and destructive cultural tide is *postmodernism.* The definition is "a late-20th-century style and concept in the arts, architecture, and criticism that represents a departure from modernism and has at its heart a general distrust of grand theories and ideologies."

In other words, the criticism and distrust of grand theories and ideologies that began with the French Enlightenment of the 18th century have, by this current point in time, completely obscured the truth leaving many in the position of living their lives—*their eternal lives*—on the basis of lies.

Postmodernism has resulted in highly sentimental, *syncretistic* (the attempt to blend various religious beliefs), and often *pluralistic* (multiple, even conflicting views about the love of God) viewpoints with no other authority base than postmodern *epistemology,* (the philosophical theory of knowledge) itself.

Is there any wonder growing numbers of people are dissatisfied, unfulfilled, confused, and more? Let's look at the source of the deception.

The Origin of Deception

The Bible reveals the one true God is self-existent. Further, although singular, God is revealed in three distinct and co-equal Persons: Father, Son, and Holy Spirit. For this reason, God is often referred to as the *Trinity.* While the use of the word Trinity is not specifically used in the Bible, the concept is evident from the beginning of the Old Testament through the end of the New Testament.

Everything that exists is created by God. Before God created humanity, He created angels. God and angels are spirit beings without any bodily form. Humankind is soul, spirit, and physical being. Our spirit is the eternal part of us that allows us to communicate with God. Our soul is the eternal, unique essence of who we are, comprised of our will, our mind, our emotions, and our distinct personality. Our bodies are temporal and simply house our spirit and soul while we dwell on earth.

God in His wisdom gave both angels and humankind free will. That is, God gave His created beings the choice to love and obey Him or not. If God had created either angels or humanity pre-programmed to love Him, that love would not be genuine, but an automated, involuntary response devoid of any real meaning.

Free will is necessary for a genuinely loving relationship. God knew by giving humanity freewill the possibility of them rejecting Him was real.

However, with foreknowledge, God determined what His response would be concerning the rejection by both angels and humans.

At some point in time, a high-ranking angel known as Lucifer (later referred to as Satan) rallied a rebellion with some of the heavenly angels. We're not told in Scripture exactly what happened, but we do know Lucifer and his followers, about one-third of the angelic hosts, were banished from heaven.[3] Satan's only desire is to dethrone God and destroy all that is important to God. When God created the first man, Adam, and the first woman, Eve, Satan saw his new opportunity.

Genesis, chapters one through three, reveals the creation of all the natural world. The creation of mankind, fashioned in God's image to live in God's loving care, was the last of God's creation efforts. Adam and Eve were the first human beings ever created. Adam was created from the dust of the ground, and Eve was fashioned from Adam's side.

Satan and his evil minions observed all God did. And knowing God's desire to enjoy a holy, loving relationship with mankind, Satan devised a wicked scheme to bring about harm to God and humanity. He appeared to Eve as a beguiling serpent. By engaging her in conversation and raising questions that appealed to Eve's natural desire, he ultimately brought her to doubt God and His intentions for humanity. Enticed by Satan, Eve willfully chose to reject God and His ways in preference for her own ways. Adam observed his wife's willful action, and he too chose to reject God and His ways.

Both Adam and Eve knew God had forewarned them if they ate the forbidden fruit, they would die. And so, they did. The moment they disobeyed God, their bodies were put on a course of physical deterioration into eventual death. With that single choice, the eternal spirits God had placed in Adam and Eve were corrupted and forever severed from enjoying the kind of pure, loving relationship they had previously known with God.

Satan's scheme of destruction was successful, and every manner of wickedness, sickness, death and destruction entered creation. This scenario is often referred to as *the curse* that resulted in a *fallen world*.

As a result, every human being born since Adam and Eve has inherited this fallen nature with the same corrupt spirit, soul, and body. This means every human being is born at enmity with God. We are doomed to eternal destruction—separated from God and all that is good.

Rejecting God is sin. Sin is both a condition every human being has inherited from Adam and Eve and behavior we continue to employ in our natural-born state.

But God ...

God's love and faithfulness—His essential nature—is independent of mankind. His love and faithfulness are continually expressed without reservation and without condition. Even when the first couple willfully rejected Him, He faithfully continued to express nothing but love and faithfulness. God *is* love. Love is His very nature—His uncompromising essence. There is nothing we can do to earn more of God's love. There is nothing we can do to earn less of God's love. God's love is constant.

Even though we are born at enmity with God—even though we are born with spirits that are dead to God and His love for us—His love is not withheld or altered by any measure—an amazing reality.

God's love is perfect. The love God lavishes upon us is distinctly different from any type of love we humans can experience on our own. God's love is holy and pure. God's love is unconditional and willful, unlike the love we humans naturally express.

God inquired of Adam and Eve what they had done, not because He didn't know. Rather, because they needed to own their action. Because of

Adam and Eve's freewill choice and to be true to Himself, God had to pronounce judgment and assure justice. He had made clear beforehand the result of eating the forbidden fruit. God's forewarning was an effort to test them, which they rejected, and in so doing, they rejected God.

Judgment came in the form of Satan being cursed more than any other being. Judgment came in the form of proclamations of suffering for Adam and Eve and all future humans to be born. Because God fashioned Adam from the dust of the earth, the ground was cursed. Eve would be the mother of all human beings, so pain in childbearing was proclaimed over her. However, at the same time God pronounced judgment and consequences, He also promised He would provide a way of redemption. God promised He would provide a *Redeemer* or *Deliverer* to offer humanity a way of escape from the ravages of sin and death. God offered a way to be *saved* from the consequences of sin. God also proclaimed the future destruction of Satan (Genesis chapter three).

God's love for us is undaunted by our rejection of Him. God's love for us is not conditioned upon our response to Him. This is proven to the uttermost in the life, death, and resurrection of Jesus. In Scripture, we read: "For while we were still weak, at the right time Christ died for the ungodly. For one will scarcely die for a righteous person—though perhaps for a good person one would dare even to die—but God shows his love for us in that while we were still *sinners* Christ died for us" (Romans 5:6-8). I emphasized the word *sinners* as that is our natural condition. Sin is the act of rejecting God and His ways. A sinner is one who is not in a right relationship with God. Because we are all born of Adam and Eve, we have all inherited the same natural-born, spiritually dead condition. Therefore, we are all born sinners.

Willful Rejection

Doubting God, rejecting His love and authority and preferring instead our own way are all natural responses of humanity. As stated above, we are born enemies of God. We've inherited the condition. That the vast numbers of people living in this postmodern culture reject God, the truth of the Bible, the reality of heaven and hell, a literal devil, and the instructions for living the best possible life is no surprise then.

Gratefully, God revealed a way of escape—a way to be restored into a right relationship with Him. Not only has God revealed the way of escape from hell, which is eternal separation from God and all that is good, but He has also personally delivered on the promise of a Redeemer in the person of *Jesus*.

God created humanity to be loved by Him—to enjoy His extravagant love. He desires for all humanity to willfully love Him—not from some perverse egotistical basis, but rather for the beautiful experience of pure and holy, mutually given love.

I don't want you to be deceived, and you don't want to be deceived. So, please reconsider what you have rejected to make certain rejection is still your true and proper response. I hope that my books in this series will help you discover and live in life-giving, absolute truth.

The last three subjects in this chapter are explored in detail in my book, *Examine Your Faith! Finding Truth in a World of Lies*.

The Witness of the Bible

The Bible, discussed in chapter one, is itself a witness to God's existence, character, will, and intentions for humanity. The Bible is the unrefuted expressed written Word of God written by men inspired by God.

Both the Old and New Testaments highlight the origin and history of creation and humanity and God's loving intervention in humanity through approximately 68AD. They also contain tremendous numbers of prophecies predicting the end times and the final apprehension of evil, which is yet to occur. Replete in all the pages of Scripture runs the constant theme of God's love for humanity and His continual intervention to redeem us, to allow us to experience His unceasing love.

No original manuscripts exist for the Bible, nor do ancient manuscripts exist for the four other major world religions—Judaism, Hinduism, Buddhism, and Islam. What we have are copies of copies. Many people have therefore understandably wondered if the Bible we have today is reliable.

Concerning the Old Testament, as mentioned in chapter one, the discovery of the Dead Sea Scrolls in 1947 provided the world with one of the most sensational discoveries of our age. More than one-third of the manuscripts and fragments of manuscripts are books of the Old Testament. These copies are older by at least *one thousand years* than the documents previously known as the oldest. This means the Bible has stronger manuscript support than any other work of classical history—including Homer, Plato, Aristotle, Caesar, and Tacitus. Scholars who have compared the earliest existing manuscripts with manuscripts written centuries later attest the Old Testament has remained virtually unaltered since the original writing.

In the case of the New Testament, we have exceptional evidence that what we have is effectively identical with the original documents. One test for accuracy is the gap in time from actual events to when the events were recorded. Compared to the documents of antiquity, the gap for the New Testament is relatively short. In the case of the writings of Euripides, the gap is around 1,600 years. For Plato, the gap is about 1,300 years. And Demosthenes' writings have a gap as low as 1,200 years.

More impressive is the timing of the writings of the entirety of the New Testament. Most of the twenty-seven books were written within twenty-five to thirty years of Christ's resurrection. This means the men who wrote the accounts and letters that make up the New Testament were alive when the documents circulated, thereby open to dispute and correction from other eyewitnesses of the life, death, and resurrection of Jesus.

As stated *Examine Your Faith! Finding Truth in a World of Lies*, "Numerous papyrus manuscripts have been found in Egypt in recent years, which confirm that the New Testament documents were already in existence in the first century."

Sir Frederic Kenyon, a former director and principal librarian of the British Museum, wrote:

> The interval then between the dates of original composition and the earliest extant [existing] evidence becomes so small as to be in fact negligible, and the last foundation for any doubt that the Scriptures have come down to us substantively as they were written had now been removed. Both the authenticity and the general integrity of the books of the New Testament may be regarded as finally established.[4]

The Bible has more objective, verifiable evidence supporting the books have not been substantively altered or amended. No other religion can make that claim regarding their document(s) of religious authority. This truth based on reality is an anchor to my faith. Clearly, as we read from Revelation 22:18-19 God will not tolerate any alteration of His Word. Jeremiah 1:12 reveals that God watches over His Word to perform it. That the Dead Sea Scrolls were intact after many years is an indication God also protects His Word.

Heaven and Hell

Heaven and hell are two separate, eternal locations where spiritual beings reside. Heaven is distinctly for all God's holy beings, and hell is the domain of all ungodly beings. Human beings are created as body, soul, and spirit. Our soul and spirit are eternal and based on our freewill choice to repent and accept God's offer of redemption or not, we will live in heaven or hell once we depart from our bodies. God's desire is not that anyone should perish [suffer complete ruin or destruction] but that all should have eternal life, (see 2 Peter 3:9). God's method to accomplish that desire was fulfilled by Jesus, the Second Person of the Trinity.

Heaven is described in the Bible as a place of beauty beyond human words where no pain or suffering exists. Hell is described as a place of endless torment.

We've already established God is love and, therefore, all He does is motivated by love. In truth, God's love is what requires Him to be just. God is the authority over all. God is both the Lawgiver and the Judge. He alone can judge in truth. God is also the One who executes the sentence. Motivated by His love for us, God has revealed what we must do to be restored into right relationship with Him and to live eternally in heaven. He has also made clear the plight of those who willfully reject Him and His ways.

The fact God has revealed He will ultimately judge all that is wicked and evil is yet another evidence of His goodness because it reveals He is just.

A Literal Devil

Earlier in this chapter under the section The Origin of Deception, I provided background about the origin of evil. Lucifer, a high-ranking angel in God's heavenly host, is the originator of all evil. Lucifer rejected God and His authority was banished from heaven and to the very end of time, he and his evil followers seek to destroy God and all that is good. In his fallen state, Lucifer is referred to as Satan.

We need to know Satan is not a power equal to God. If that were the case, all creation would suffer the effects of Satan and God in battle eternally. God has revealed His plan to put an end to all that is evil in the fullness of time when all humans planned by God have been born and given an opportunity for salvation. Make no mistake, the enemy of God is very real, responsible for all that is evil and the influencer of all those who remain in sin. But, thanks to Jesus, Satan is already a defeated foe.

The real and certain hope Jesus made available for anyone who wants hope is the topic of the next chapter.

CHAPTER FOUR

The Offer of Hope

Although He had been willfully rejected, God not only promised a Redeemer for mankind because of His love, He personally *became* the Redeemer in the person of Jesus, the Son of God. God's desire was not for humanity to suffer or be eternally separated from Him and everything that is good. So, the *Triune Godhead*, the Father, the Son, and the Holy Spirit, conferred, and God the Son willingly gave up His rightful place in heaven for a time to take on human form. The plan Jesus fulfilled in His life, death, and resurrection is the promised *offer* of redemption, also referred to as salvation, for anyone who chooses to place their faith in Jesus as their personal Savior and Lord. God has made all humanity an offer of hope through Jesus. But, everyone must choose to receive salvation or not—to respond to God's call and offer of redemption.

Jesus is the clear and certain hope for all creation. The promise God made thousands of years ago was fulfilled in the unique person of Jesus.

God made a promise to all humanity beginning with the first man, Adam, and the first woman, Eve, to provide a way of redemption—a way of escaping our estrangement from God and our eternal destiny in hell. All who believed in this promise and looked forward to the promise being fulfilled—believing God for His word—received the promise by faith. All who believe the promise looking back to its fulfillment in Christ, receive the promise by faith. To be redeemed and restored is simply a matter of faith, believing God for His word—His promise. His promise to us living in the New Testament time is to believe God for His promise fulfilled in the person of Jesus.

The promise fulfilled in Jesus is the single greatest demonstration of love the world has ever known.

God has completely provided the offer of hope for anyone who desires in the Person of Jesus. But to those who consider themselves enlightened, the truth of God and the hope found in Christ is considered foolishness. From their human understanding they erroneously reject the gospel of Jesus since the gospel does not fit human reason or expectation.

Something we must understand is God doesn't send people to hell. God offers redemption. Those who willfully reject God's offer of redemption— who reject Jesus—choose hell for themselves. Choosing death or choosing life has been a choice for every human being beginning with Adam and Eve.

The Historical Reality of Jesus

Jesus was and is the promised Redeemer, born of a virgin named Mary. According to the Bible, God *overshadowed* Mary and miraculously united the human egg with the Holy Spirit, allowing Jesus to be conceived. This made Him both fully human and fully God. Jesus, therefore, had two distinct natures. Being fully human, He could die for us as our substitute. Being fully God, He could save us.

Although fully God, Jesus, in His human nature, was and is the most unique of all human beings. John 1:14 explains "And the Word [Jesus, the Son of God] became flesh [Son of Man] and dwelt among us." Jesus' most often used reference to Himself was *Son of Man.* God is not distant and removed from our mortal existence. He has experienced every joy and every sorrow known to man as a man. He lived in the human condition being tempted by every temptation known to man, yet He did not sin.

The way Jesus refrained from committing sin was by remaining in communication with and obeying God the Father as we read in John 8:28 and elsewhere in Scriptures. Jesus came to this earth as the Redeemer of mankind, motivated by tremendous love. And this love allowed Him to suffer unimaginable torture by the very people He came to save. He was falsely accused, arrested, improperly tried and sentenced to death by way of crucifixion. Before His death, He was mercilessly beaten until His appearance was no longer was recognizable as human. His hands and feet were nailed to a cross, and the cross was erected so that He would die a slow and excruciating death. Yet, He never surrendered His mission. He willingly suffered all He did. He bled and died so that you would have a way to be restored to God and His love.

Consider that God, in the form of Jesus, suffered on your behalf. First, He willingly gave up His rightful place in heaven and took upon Himself human existence. God is not distant and removed from our mortal existence. He has experienced every joy and every sorrow known to man as a man. He lived in the human condition, being tempted by every temptation known to man, yet He did not sin. The ultimate expression of God's love for you was demonstrated by Jesus. Jesus, who knew no sin, became sin for us so we could have a path back to God. God revealed His love for you by the very life blood of Jesus—God in human form.

By faith in the life, death, and resurrection of Jesus as the Redeemer, anyone who desires can be saved from sin and the eternal death sin brings, according to the Bible. Through faith in Jesus, a person is restored to a spiritually alive condition and enjoys a personal relationship with God.

Faith in Jesus literally transforms a person's natural-born, dead spirit condition to a newly created *born-again* spirit that never before existed. This new spirit condition is pure and holy and able to relate to God in every way possible. Scriptures teach, "For our sake, he [God] made him [Jesus] to be sin who knew no sin so that in him [Jesus] we might become the righteousness of God" (1 Corinthians 5:21).

Believing in Jesus, the Son of God, as your personal Savior or Redeemer from sin, not only restores you to a loving relationship with God the Father, but also allows you to receive God's Holy Spirit to indwell you—to enable you to learn how to live your new life in Christ. God does not save us then leave us on our own. No, He personally takes up residence in our being through the Person of the Holy Spirit.

Faith in Jesus allows you to escape the final Judgment Day without personal condemnation. Placing faith in Jesus brings many, many benefits and full access to all the promises of God. The Bible reveals an abundance of benefits including love, peace, joy, freedom, overcoming power, provision, health, long life, a grand and divine purpose for living, and more.

In addition to the Bible, there are many extra-biblical texts that document the birth, life, teachings, miraculous healings, death and bodily resurrection of Jesus. Few deny Jesus was a historical person. However, the view of many people runs contrary not only to the Bible but to much of documented history and the over five hundred *eyewitnesses* of His resurrected state. Many self-professed enlightened people today claim Jesus was a good teacher, perhaps a prophet. Many state Jesus is to be revered in the same way as Buddha or Muhammad. Such statements reveal they have not taken the time to study the facts, and for that reason, they are sadly deceived. You can find more compelling reasons to believe in Jesus in the first book in this series, *Examine Your Faith! Finding Truth in a World of Lies.*

You are Unique and Precious to God

Scriptures reveal God knew you before you were ever knit together in your mother's womb—before you were formed, (Psalm 139:13-14). You are not simply a natural by-product of conception. You were *intended* by God to be born into this world with your own unique personality, talents, and abilities. You are unique. There never has been, nor will there ever be a duplicate of you. Your unique fingerprints demonstrate God set you apart from all others ever born. God *distinctly* delights over *you.*

We are each unique, yet made in God's image. That we are each distinctly different, and each made in God's image, helps us understand how vastly multifaceted our God is. Your unique being is something to take the time to fully grasp.

Because of the deception of humanity, we are prone to compete, compare, and contrast ourselves with others, which only leads to dissatisfaction and worse. But, with the firm understanding that each person is unique with their own place in God's plan, with their own purpose and destiny, there is no reason to do so. How can one unique being be compared to another unique being? Each is unique. On the contrary, we have every reason to celebrate our God-given distinctions.

Discovering Your Created Purpose

When we find ourselves anxious, restless, and otherwise dissatisfied with the direction our life seems to be going, we should recognize that as evidence we've veered off course and are not operating according to our created purpose. One's God-given purpose is often referred to as their *call* or *calling*. Discovering your created purpose is not difficult, yet doing so is something too few people accomplish. To help you, I've provided some guidelines for discovering your created purpose and how to best function in your calling.

The first thing you should experience is an excitement in knowing you are called by God for a specific purpose in your life. You are unique, so the contribution you can make on earth for God's kingdom is unique. Collectively, all believers are referred to as the *Body of Christ*. And just as the human body has many members, we need each part of the physical body to do its part for the entire body to properly function. The apostle Paul wrote of how we are to experience unity with diversity as one body in 1 Corinthians chapter 12. He wrote in verse 18 that "God arranged the members in the body, each one of them, as he chose." Your created purpose was established by God. When you live accordingly, you not only please Him but enjoy personal fulfillment otherwise not available. Additionally, living according to your call benefits others.

When discovering your call, you need to consider both your *natural talents* and the *spiritual gifts* God has given you. Spiritual gifts will be discussed more particularly in the next chapter. Your natural talents are abilities you have to do things well, and that bring you pleasure. More about recognizing your natural talents is provided in chapter eight.

Transformed and United, We Change the World

All who place their faith in Jesus are to be united in God's love and purpose. As we read the Bible and learn of God's perfect instructions for living in what is good and true and we willingly cooperate with the Holy Spirit, we are indeed changed. We are transformed from the inside out.

All who believe in Jesus as their personal Savior and Lord are collectively referred to as *the Church* or *Christ's Body*. Believers in Jesus are commissioned by Jesus to be His disciples and to make disciples of people of all nations. This means we have a part to play in God's plan to gather in all who belong to Him.

Additionally, motivated by His love for you, God continually arranges situations and circumstances so you can discover the truth about Him and His will for your life. He longs for you to discover more and more truth and for you to be robed in the righteousness of Christ. He longs for you to learn how to be the victorious, new creature you can be through faith in Jesus. God has a created purpose for you, one only you can fulfill. That purpose is your God-given destiny if accepted. And Christ's life, death, and resurrection have secured everything you need to fulfill your destiny. How to discover your purpose is addressed beginning in chapter six.

As each of us seeks to grow in our new spirit beings, we will be transformed.

Transformed by the Love of God

When a person places his or her faith in Jesus, their spirit is completely regenerated. Your ability to communicate with God is open as never before. Plus, you have the indwelling of God's Holy Spirit to guide you. John 14:17 and 1 Corinthians 6:19-20 are just two passages in Scripture that state whenever a person chooses to repent from sin and place their faith in Jesus as their personal Savior, God causes the Holy Spirit to *indwell* the believer. Every believer mysteriously receives the indwelling of the Holy Spirit, the third Person of the Triune Godhead (Ephesians 1:14). The indwelling of the Holy Spirit is the guarantee of our eternal inheritance through faith in Christ.

There remains a problem, however. We are still living in our earthly bodies in this fallen world and experience natural carnal desires. Our body will do whatever our mind allows even if those actions are not consistent with the will of God. That is why the apostle Paul stresses the importance of *renewing our minds*. We renew our minds by replacing the carnal, earthly thoughts of our *unregenerate* self with the life-giving truths of God's written Word. As we do this, our bodily lusts and desires will be put under submission to our new spirit in Christ. Those who know and love Jesus will want to keep His commands, knowing that keeping His commands will transform us more and more into His image.

Everything good is from God. If you want to experience the abundant, victorious life Christ died to provide for you, simply place your faith in Jesus. Perhaps you'd like to do that now? If so, in your own words, simply agree with God about your natural, sin-born condition. Thank God for sending Jesus and declare you are willing to repent. Acknowledge you are placing your faith in Jesus as your personal Savior and Lord. With just these simple words expressed from a genuine heart, you can be confident your redemption is sure. When anyone places his or her faith in Jesus, their name is written in the *Lamb's Book of Life*, also referred to as the *Book of Life*, along with all the others who have placed their faith in Jesus. The Bible reveals the Lamb's Book of Life is the record of the ones who will enter the "holy city, Jerusalem" (Revelation 21:10) and who will live forever in heaven with God. This is cause to celebrate!

Sealed by the Blood of Jesus

The Old Testament animal sacrifice system was established by God to provide a covering for sin and was a demonstration of the *covenant* God made with man for all who obeyed and believed in Him and His promises. Christians believe this sacrificial system also provided a *type* of the ultimate sacrifice—Jesus, the promised Redeemer/Deliverer. That John the Baptist, who was a contemporary of Jesus, understood this is illustrated when he referred to Jesus as the *Lamb of God* (reference John 1:29).

Old Testament believers looked forward to the fulfillment of God's promise while New Testament believers look back to the promise fulfilled in Jesus.

Hebrews 9:22 states, " … without the shedding of blood there is no forgiveness of sins." Scripture reveals that once Adam and Eve confessed their disobedience, God covered their bodies with *animal skin.* Hence, God Himself shed the first blood to *cover* sin until the time of the promised Redeemer whose sacrifice would *cleanse* believers from sin.

God is unable to lie. God is unable to go back on His promises—His Word. He had declared without the shedding of blood there could be no remission of sin. And that's precisely why Jesus came to this earth—to become the supreme and final sacrifice, shedding His blood, sealing the fulfillment of the promise of God to provide reconciliation forever.

Rest in God's Covenant

J. I. Packer wrote, "God's love is an exercise of His goodness toward individual sinners whereby, having identified himself with their welfare, he has given his Son to be their Savior, and now brings them to know and enjoy him in a *covenant* relation"[1] (emphasis added).

A covenant is a binding agreement or contract. In terms of Scripture, a covenant as instituted by God is a contract. In the Bible, a covenant is an agreement between God and His people in which God makes promises to His people and, usually, requires certain conduct from them.

"Using covenants," writes Matt Slick of Christian Apologetics and Research Ministry, "is how God communicates to us, redeems us, and guarantees us eternal life in Jesus. He does this because a covenant is a promise, and God's promises cannot be broken since they rest in His infinite, pure character. The Bible is a covenant document. The Old and New Testaments are really old and new covenants. The word 'testament' is Latin for covenant. All covenants in the Bible between God and man are originated by God and are an act of his grace."[2]

Instituted by God, a covenant is not given so much to emphasize the *legality* of the agreement as much as it is to emphasize the *relationship* of the parties involved. And for this, we should be exceedingly grateful because, repeatedly throughout all history, humankind has failed to live up to our part of the covenant. Even so, God has never failed to deliver on His part.

There are some covenants or promises, such as the second coming of Jesus, that require nothing from us to ultimately enjoy the benefits of the promise. But there are other promises that do require satisfying specific conditions. The conditions for such promises are not obscure. They are plain and given to us in Scripture so we will know what we must do to receive the benefit. For example, if we want to be in right relationship with God the Father and enjoy all the good gifts extending from His love, the condition we must satisfy is to believe in and receive Jesus by faith as our personal Lord and Savior.

Study of the Old Testament is indispensable in a Christian's journey. Reading the Old Testament allows us to embrace the rich heritage of God's continual loving intervention in the lives of His beloved humanity—often expressed in stern discipline and even judgments in a just response to the people's actions.

In Luke 16:16, Jesus made clear the *Law and the Prophets* were proclaimed until John the Baptist. The Law and the prophecies concerning the *Messiah* or the Christ heralded until the advent of Jesus. Jesus stressed He did not come to abolish the Law, rather to fulfill it. The Old Testament would always remain inspired and, moreover, Scripture was fulfilled which is not something to disregard.

As you learn more about the life and times in the Old Testament era, you will become exceedingly grateful you live in the New Testament era. In the New Testament, we learn Jesus' life, death, and resurrection have completely satisfied the debt of sin once and for all. His perfect existence means He has fulfilled all the Law and the Prophets, thereby concluding the Old Testament era of Law and ushering in the New Testament era of grace.

As He hung on the cross, Jesus' last words before declaring He was commending His Spirit to the Father, were "It is finished!" You and I are privileged to live in the New Testament era of God's grace with all glory and gratitude belonging to Jesus alone, Amen.

God is Faithful Even When We are Unfaithful

Of the many attributes of God, one pertinent at this point is God is *immutable*. He cannot change. He is the same yesterday, today, and tomorrow. We need never fear God changing His mind or acting inconsistently with His revealed will and character. This one attribute gives me the supreme confidence to surrender my trust to Him with all abandon.

One of my favorite books in the Old Testament is Hosea because the story so perfectly reveals God's immutability in His love for us. The message of Hosea is of God's love motivating His overwhelming mercy for

His people. The story in Hosea reveals the repeated unfaithfulness of God's people with a number of images from family and nature. Israel is like a promiscuous wife, an indifferent mother, an illegitimate child, an ungrateful son, a stubborn heifer, a silly dove, a luxuriant vine, and grapes in the wilderness. Yet Israel's unfaithfulness and obstinacy are not enough to exhaust God's redeeming love. Recurrent themes include: 1.) the unfolding list of acts and attitudes that disappoint God; 2.) a picture of what people who reject God can expect to receive from Him; and 3.) evidences of God's love and grace toward people who do not deserve them.[3]

While the book describes the condition of God's people in the years 786-746 BC, the text is a depiction of how people repeatedly responded to God throughout all ages. God is represented by Hosea, the husband, whereas Israel, or God's people, is represented by Gomer, the wife.

Hosea, an Old Testament prophet, was known by all to be a righteous man of God. Yet, he was instructed *by God* to very publicly seek out and marry a *known* prostitute. So, he did. He married Gomer, a woman who was known for her innumerable adulterous liaisons. Through the prophet, God relays to us we are as a prostitute toward Him. In our relationship with Him, we often commit spiritual adultery.

The story of Hosea reveals God's unconditional love and faithfulness, illustrated in contrast to the sinful harlotry of His people—who are so easily enticed away from Him by the things of this world, thereby committing spiritual adultery.

God initiated His covenant with people He knew were unfaithful. He knew we would reject Him in preference for our own ways—repeatedly. But even when we are unfaithful, He remains faithful to His part of the covenant.

If you've known betrayal in a loving relationship, then you know the deep pain of the heart. God is a feeling being. When we reject Him, He is not unfazed. We read in Scripture that God experiences grief at the actions of His people. While humans find expressing anger or severing a relationship with a person who betrays us acceptable, this is not how God responds. His love for His own far outweighs every other emotion, and so, His love motivates all He does.

God's mercy does not mean there are no consequences for our choices contrary to God's will. Rather, His mercy simply means we don't get the full consequences we deserve. There are still consequences for our choices.

Distinguishing Love from Approval

The distinction between God's love and God's approval is important. Just as earthly parents withhold good gifts from disobedient children, God will discipline us. Discipline does not mean love has been withheld. Quite the contrary, good parents and our good God discipline us *out of* love. Hebrews 12:6-11 reveals:

> For the Lord disciplines the one he loves, and chastises every son whom he receives. It is for discipline that you have to endure. God is treating you as sons. For what son is there whom his father does not discipline? If you are left without discipline, in which all have participated, then you are illegitimate children and not sons. Besides this, we have had earthly fathers who disciplined us and we respected them. Shall we not much more be subject to the Father of spirits and live? For they disciplined us for a short time as it seemed best to them, but he disciplines us for our good, that we may share his holiness. For the moment all discipline seems painful rather than pleasant, but later it

yields the peaceful fruit of righteousness to those who have been trained by it.

Many people find certain promises of God to seem unduly restrictive and, therefore, conclude *God must be a killjoy*. Nothing could be further from the truth. God ordained several different week-long feasts to celebrate different holidays. God created humanity with the ability to laugh and have fun. God created humanity with the joy of sex in marriage. When humanity seeks to enter any activity in a manner inconsistent with God's instruction, the activity becomes perverted. For example, God instructed that sex is to be enjoyed within the confines of marriage, not to be a killjoy, but as a matter of protecting us. Sexually transmitted diseases, birth defects, and long-lasting emotional and spiritual problems are the consequences of having sex outside of marriage. Another example is keeping the Sabbath day, which is Sunday in the New Testament era. God knows precisely how He created us and what is best for our health—body, soul, and spirit. Keeping the Sabbath is to set aside the day to rest from our daily work-related activities and make a point of being focused on God in the assembly of fellow believers.

As already stated, everything God does is motivated by His love for us. All His *restrictions* are for our good, even if they don't seem to be to us. Jesus said, "You are my friends if you do what I command you" (John 15:14). Another way to say this is "If you really know Me, then you will love Me, and keeping my commandments will be your first choice, because you know I only want the best for you, at all times."

If a person genuinely or properly knows God, they can't help but choose to love Him and embrace all His ways. We desire God and His love because we have a great need for Him and all He offers. He is our Creator, and we are fashioned in His image. He desires a relationship with us, so we are created to desire a relationship with Him.

In the next chapter, you will read real-life examples of lives and circumstances amazingly transformed by God's love and grace.

PART TWO

EMBRACING LOVE

"For God so loved the world, that he gave his only Son, that whoever believes in him should not perish but have eternal life."

John 3:16

CHAPTER FIVE

God's Intervening Love

I am nothing like the person I was before I gave my life to Jesus. My story is in the first book of this series, *Examine Your Faith! Finding Truth in a World of Lies*. In short, I encountered what was then the most devastating crisis I'd ever known. My whole world collapsed, and the foundation I'd based my life on crumbled and vanished.

In my utter agony, I vaguely remembered the Jesus a Sunday school teacher taught me about when I was very little. In my crisis, having no place else to turn, I called out to God. I basically said to Him that if He was really who the Sunday school teacher proclaimed—if He was a good and loving God who could make something better of my life, then I was willing to give myself to Him without reservation. I needed someone greater than me to guide me. I needed Him to be real and make something better of my life because, on my own, I'd repeatedly proven all I could do is make a mess of my life.

The instant I concluded my deepest and most genuine prayer for God to become my Lord and Savior, I was forever changed. I could sense a profound difference within. Utterly amazed, I sat in silence. No longer crying uncontrollably. No longer overcome with grief. But sitting instead in overwhelming awe.

Many things in my life were transformed in an instant. Certainly, my spirit was made new, but so were the joy and peace and hope I felt. There were many other things that were transformed over a period of time. Some matters took time because they were habits I needed to change. Other issues took time because I was learning how to live my life as a new creature in Christ.

Imagine a person learning late in life the poverty and oppression they'd always known, was not their true identity. Rather, they were a child of the King, part of the royal family, entitled to all the benefits of the palace, and joint heir to *all* the power, authority, and possessions that belonged to the King. That is exactly what happened in my life, and what happens in the life of every person, young or old, who sincerely places their faith in Jesus.

Before that night when I cried out to God with genuine abandon, I had tried to have Jesus as my Savior to keep me from hell, but I wanted to maintain lordship of my own life. That is, until I found I needed all of Jesus. And as I've learned, Jesus wanted all of me too.

When Jesus is truly Lord of your life, you have every solution to every problem at your disposal. That's not to say you won't suffer in this life. But when you suffer, you have the victory of Christ's life, which demonstrated God's love to overcome His suffering. So long as we live in this fallen world, we will be subject to the ravages of sin and evil. But when we operate our lives consistent with our new identity in Christ, we have kingdom strategies for victory and for enjoying the abundant life Christ died to provide us. When we are entirely submitted to Jesus, we can expect to be transformed more and more—we can expect to continually be perfected—growing in God's grace. And we can expect to be able to joyfully go through trials because of our knowledge of our place in His kingdom.

God's Unexpected Demonstrations of His Love

How to best tap into Christ's promised victory is the topic of the second book in this series, *Renew Your Hope! Remedy for Personal Breakthroughs*. To enjoy the promise of redemption, we must believe in and receive Jesus. This is how we work with God, according to His plan to bring about His will. We're in a partnership.

But, there are times beyond initial conversion when, through no effort of our own, God simply shows up and lavishes His love on us. He might give some unexpected reassurance to us, He might suddenly impart some wisdom or insight needed to solve a problem, or He might work miraculously in our lives to spare us pain and suffering. He might show up in any of these ways or any number of other ways. But no matter how God reveals Himself, the revelation impacts us for a lifetime.

There are times when God reveals Himself in such a way people acquire *experiential knowledge* of Him. Such an experience seals the certainty about God's love. At the time of this writing, there are an inordinate number of "Jesus sightings" in the Middle East. In these sightings, He's most commonly referred to as "The Man in White." Conduct an online search for the phrase "Jesus appearing in the Middle East," and note the many accounts of thousands of Muslims "seeing" Jesus. Most of these encounters are to help people realize the truth about Jesus as the Son of God, who offers redemption to anyone who desires. But besides conversion, there are many other reasons God decides to make Himself known—many reasons He would opt to miraculously intervene in the lives of His people.

Following are several true stories of people who have encountered an unexpected demonstration of God's love. Some of the stories are dramatic; some of the stories are not, but all the events are real and especially uplifting.

God's Love Imparts Supernatural Insight

I served as Teaching/Director for Community Bible Study—an interdenominational, independent Bible study. We would often have luncheons where the leaders and our children would enjoy potluck meals at one of our homes.

All our children were out of school for the summer, and a swimming party for the kids seemed a good idea to most. I recall being quite hesitant about having so many children, some of whom were quite young, in and around a pool. I even voiced my concern only to hear all the other mothers dismiss my concerns, causing me to feel I was overly cautious. I agreed to have the pool party, and we made our plans.

After lunch and equipping the children for their swim time by putting on life jackets and arm-floaties, the splashing began. We moms were seated at a table with a view of the pool, but far enough away we could hear ourselves talk above the squeals of the kids and the splashing of water. At some point, in a mindless state, not consciously choosing to turn my head, I looked toward the pool and very specifically focused in on my four-year-old son. Almost like some sort of outside homing device was operating to cause my eyes to focus directly on my son without having to search for him among all the many children.

He was facing me in the shallow end of the pool. His blue eyes were wider than ever, and all that showed; his nose was under the surface of the water. Without a word and with inexplicable power, I ran over and into the pool to grab my son. I pulled him up and out of the pool and sat down with him on the cement. He and I were both horribly shaken. I trembled and cried at the thought of what could have happened to my son.

The other children were happily playing, completely unaware of my son's plight. The sad reality of drowning is there is no warning sound from a person who can't swim. I pulled my son toward me, hugging him. He was clearly remorseful, knowing I told him he had to wear the life jacket and floaties. He had taken off the floaties and life jacket I'd placed on him, wanting to be like the bigger boys who knew how to swim. Had God not caused me to look directly at my son so I could act without delay, my precious son would have drowned.

I praise God to this day for His supernatural help and sparing my son, along with the knowledge I get to live in God's loving care daily. I believe because I was trusting God to be involved with every detail of my daily life, I was and am able to *hear* God when He is aware of a situation, and I am not.

God's Tender Love Transcends Rage

Heidi McLaughlin an International speaker, author and Bible teacher, shares her story of a time when God's loving assurance pierced through her confrontation with God.

With pounding heart, I ventured into our walk-in closet to change from my church clothes into something more casual and comfortable. My husband, Dick, had died three days prior, and thus far, I had been unable to face the emotions of seeing his clothes in the closet hanging next to mine. I hadn't given *any* thought I would be met with his personal scent in that closet. Reality was bitter-sweet.

I stood and marveled at Dick's shirts, always lined up so perfectly. Except for one sleeve. The shirt must have been the last one he had worn before he went out to play basketball. In his hurry, he hadn't hung it up quite properly. My eyes stayed glued to that one blue sleeve. *This must be the last shirt he wore and didn't have time to put away properly. He will never come back to wear this shirt. He will never again wear any of these shirts or walk into this closet.*

The forced and stoic composure I had faked at church that morning completely crumbled, and I fell to the floor on my knees. Dick's death finally hit me. He would never come back. I was alone.

Sobbing uncontrollably and furious, I pounded the closet room floor. My body shook, and hot tears streamed down my face. I screamed at God, "Why did you let this happen? I've spent years honoring you and serving you! You said you would never leave me or forsake me. Where are you now? When I really need you, I feel you have completely abandoned me."

In the middle of my explosive anger, I experienced unusual warmth, that felt like warm oil flowing over my head, down into my arms, through my whole body, then down to the tip of my toes. My anger and shaking stopped. Peace flowed through me as though I had been held and hugged. What I experienced could only be the Holy Spirit, the Comforter Jesus said He would send.

Without a shadow of a doubt, I knew God's Spirit was comforting me in that closet. He knew my excruciating pain and was there to comfort and give me new strength. He was faithful to His promise. "Never will I leave you; never will I forsake you" (Hebrews 13:5 NIV). I will never forget that holy encounter, experiencing God's lavish love.

The days, weeks, and months ahead were dark, and my grief was beyond any pain I had ever experienced. But having and recalling that very personal "closet experience" carried me through. God had not abandoned me on this unexpected and lonely pathway. He met me in my rage with nothing but reassuring love—the same love I rely on daily. Twenty-one years have elapsed since Dick's passing. Even though Dick left a gnawing void in my heart, I am comforted knowing we are both still connected in spirit through God's amazing love."

Heidi McLaughlin and her new husband live in Kelowna, British Columbia, Canada. Her website is: www.heartconnection.ca

God's Love Surpasses Rejection

Darren Canning, an itinerant revival preacher, shares how God's love remained faithful even during a long season of his rejecting God.

When I was a boy, my idea of God was formed through attending church with my parents. When their divorce occurred, we stopped going to church. However, my grandparents took me once or twice a year.

At fifteen I had become a Christian. I later went to Bible College and became a pastor. I got married at age twenty and truly thought my life was on track with God. However, when I was twenty-one, my ministry fell apart when the pastor I worked with kicked me out of the church over a minor disagreement about theology. The pain of that moment is hard to put into words. I had been prophesying a revival was going to take place in that church, and three months after I was kicked out, revival started. I thought *If the kind of God you are rewards those that hurt people, I want nothing to do you or your church.*

Following that experience, I immersed myself on a path to earn both a BA in Philosophy and a BA in Political Science. I finished two degrees in five years. At that point, I considered myself an agnostic and even dabbled in witchcraft. I became a womanizer and drank all the time.

My wife and I both struggled with depression and anxiety and often fought like cats and dogs. We had two small daughters who were three and six years old, and I spent most of my free time with them. After eight years of marriage, we decided to divorce. In the one year of separation, I only saw my daughters about seven days out of an entire year. Their absence was very hard on me.

The darkness in my life was so intense I rarely had a moment where I did not feel tormented with suicidal thoughts. I would literally hear voices taunting me to kill myself. I would often see spirits in my room like dark shadows. I knew they were there, but I still refused to turn back to God.

I couldn't see anything good about my life. I had read many books about the afterlife that painted it as simply a place that you disappear into. I believed I came from darkness and would return to it. There would be no consequences for my death. I would simply fade out into eternity—like gas disappearing into the sky.

Then the day came when I prepared my closet so I could hang myself. Just before my planned suicide, I called my mother. She was now a committed Christian. She tried to talk me out of killing myself, but I cut her off and said, "Mom I am only calling to say goodbye. Please tell my daughters and my sister that I love them very much, and I love you, Mom."

She hung up the phone and later told me she'd thought *There are two things I can do. I can call the police but they will not make it in time, or I can dance and start singing AS FOR ME AND MY HOUSE WE WILL SERVE THE LORD.* As she did this, a great peace came over her.

I went into my closet and placed the cable cord that I'd tied to the bar around my neck. I dropped to my knees and could feel the cord cutting off my ability to breathe. I started to black out and see stars. At that moment, I heard God speak for the first time in years. He said, "What are you doing? I have a plan for your life." I was shocked and tried to convince myself my own mind was speaking. I moved my body so the pressure around my neck would increase. Again, I started to black out and see stars and again, I heard God speak saying, "What are you doing? I have a plan for your life."

I was scared now. *If God is speaking to me then perhaps there is a hell, and I might be heading toward it.* I feebly jumped up, somehow got out of the cable noose and ran out of the closet to my bed. I stood on the bed, and in a frenzy, started jumping up and down waving my fist at the ceiling and at God. I said, "How dare you speak to me after all of these years!" Immediately, I passed out and fell asleep.

That night, I had a dream encounter with God where I experienced His unconditional love. Years ago, I'd learned the truth God's love is unconditional. But that night, I experienced His love. And when I awoke, I knew God had a plan for my life.

Although I had had an amazing encounter, I took two more years to recommit my life to Christ. Since 2004, God's plan is being fulfilled in my life daily. And now, fourteen years later, I am still going strong. I was remarried to my wife, Lydia, and we now have five children together. My deepest privilege is to travel and help others realize the eternal, unconditional, transforming love of God.

Darren and his family live in Ottawa Valley, Canada and travel to minister where invited. More at www.darrencanning.com

God's Love Defies Natural Laws

Carol Graham, an award-winning author, talk show host, international speaker, and a certified health coach, shares how God's love sent angels of protection.

When my husband, Paul, was twelve years old, his father asked him to steer a Jeep he was towing with a car and a long chain.

They stopped to fill up with gas, and Paul went into the corner store to buy some candy. He was deciding how much to spend when he heard what seemed like an audible voice say, "There is going to be a car accident, but you are going to be okay." He spun around to see who had spoken to him but saw no one.

He was afraid to tell his father, so he got into the Jeep and piled blankets and pillows up next to him in hopes of diving under them in case of an accident. Several miles down the road, his dad turned onto a gravel road where a grader was leveling two ridges of piled up gravel. Paul was trying to steer over the two-foot-high ridges when the Jeep began to sway out of control. The chain snapped, and the Jeep rolled. Paul was thrown out the driver's window and into the ditch. The entire weight of the vehicle landed on top of him upside down. The impact was so hard the Jeep bounced up about ten feet into the air over the fence and landed on its wheels in the neighboring field. Several of Paul's teeth were knocked out, but amazingly he had only suffered some scrapes and bruises—no broken bones.

When they looked over the situation, his dad, shocked, made a strange observation. "Look how large the dent is in the roof of the Jeep where it landed on top of you. That is sure odd, how in the world could this be? There is no way your body could have made that large of a dent." Years later, God revealed to Paul that not only had He warned him of the accident, but He had protected him as well. An angel created that large dent in the Jeep by taking the full impact for him.

As a teenager, Paul lived in a town that had many steep hills. One day, he and his buddies were speeding down one of them on their motorcycles and were almost at the intersection when Paul realized he had no brakes.

He had two choices: go through the red light or make a right-hand turn. He negotiated the turn but hit an oncoming car at forty miles per hour.

What happened next defied reality. His buddies stood and watched this unfold as if in slow motion. The bike hit the car head-on. Paul shot straight up into the air. He was held there by unseen hands as he watched his motorcycle being demolished. He looked down and smiled at his friends, who were staring up in disbelief. After the screeching of brakes had stopped, Paul was set gently on his feet. Paul walked over to the driver of the car to see if he was all right. Once again, what might have been meant for evil was turned into good. Paul couldn't help but wonder if this was the same guardian angel who had protected him before. Both of Paul's buddies who were with him that day asked Jesus into their hearts.

Carol has five grandchildren and has rescued over thirty dogs. Her ministry offers hope and encouragement. batteredhope.blogspot.com

No One is Beyond God's Love

In all honesty, as you read the preceding testimonies, did you have any thought that God works in the lives of others, but you are somehow beyond the limits for God to work in your life? If you're inclined to think you are beyond God's love and blessings, you have succumbed to deception. You are who God says you are, not who the world or the devil says you are. A proper realignment of your identity will establish your God-intended destiny.

You are reading this book because you believe there is something more for you in life, right? You want to sense your personal significance. You want to discover your unique purpose and contribution to the world. Well, you never will find those things until you first discover God's love for you that is *independent* of all others. God loves you distinctly, and He's calling you into a deeper relationship with Him.

God is love. Jesus is our real and certain hope. His life, death, and resurrection open the way for us to be restored into a right relationship with God. Faith is the heart, soul, and mindset that allows you to enter God's perfect love. Faith is trust and belief based on enough objective, verifiable evidence to allow you to confidently anticipate what is not yet known or manifest.

The apostle Paul is attributed with writing more books than any other author in the New Testament. His personal conversion from a leader in Judaism to an apostle of Jesus Christ is exceedingly compelling. His name at birth was Saul, and he was known as Saul of *Tarsus,* the region where he was born in what we know as southern Turkey today.

Saul grew and became a *Pharisee* in Jerusalem. A Pharisee was a recognized religious leader among the Jewish people. A man had to be at least thirty years of age and satisfy several other requirements to be accepted among the Pharisees.

As we can read in Acts chapter nine, after the crucifixion and resurrection of Jesus Christ, Saul swore to wipe out the new church, which was then referred to as *The Way.* With letters of authority from the high priest in hand, Saul zealously arrested any followers of Jesus he found. On the road leading to Damascus, Saul was suddenly struck down by a blinding light. Acts 9:4 reveals that Saul heard a voice ask, "Saul, Saul, why are you persecuting me?" In response, Saul asked who was speaking to him. The voice replied, "I am Jesus, whom you are persecuting. But rise and enter the city, and you will be told what you are to do." (Acts 9:5-6)

The men with Saul heard the sound but did not see the vision of the risen Christ that Saul beheld. Saul was blinded, so they led him by the hand into Damascus to a man named Judas, on Straight Street. Saul and his companions stayed with Judas for three days. During this time, Saul neither ate nor drank anything.

Sometime during the three days, the resurrected Christ appeared in a vision to a member of The Way in Damascus. His name was Ananias. Jesus told him to go to Saul. Ananias feared for his life, knowing Saul's reputation for persecuting believers.

Jesus again told Ananias to go to Saul, and He also assured Ananias that Saul was His chosen vessel to deliver the *gospel* (good news of Jesus the Redeemer) to the *Gentiles*. So, Ananias went to Saul and found him praying for help. Ananias laid his hands on Saul, telling him Jesus had sent him to restore his sight, and that Saul might be filled with the Holy Spirit.

Something like scales fell from Saul's eyes, and his vision was restored. Immediately, Saul arose and was baptized into The Way. Saul ate, regained his strength and began his new life in Christ. Since the name Saul was a Jewish name Saul decided to use his Roman name, Paul, after his conversion. Paul was a name the *Gentiles* were accustomed to, which allowed him an easier reception.[1] Gentile is the term given to all the people were not Jewish. Saul was born a Jew and a citizen of Rome. After a time, the Christian church leadership recognized Paul as an apostle or important leader, and as such, Paul did a great deal to spread the gospel far and wide among Gentiles.

No matter how far you've been from believing in and receiving Jesus as your personal Savior, no matter how violently you have lived, if your heart becomes so inclined, nothing can separate you from God's love and plan for your life. Coming to recognize God's love for him is what transformed Pau's life—a man who had been a zealous murderer of Jesus' followers.

Conversion or transformation is very real. When you place your faith in Jesus, you are transformed once for all time, and you enter the process of *sanctification*, so you are continually transformed more and more into the righteousness of Christ.

In the next chapter, we'll explore more fully who God says you are, how to discover your God-intended purpose and how to step into the personal, significant contribution to the world God had planned for you before you were born.

CHAPTER SIX

God's Purpose for You

When I found John Rinehart's excellent and inspiring article about God's view of you as revealed in the Bible, I invited him to be a contributor to this book. What follows is John's article, *What Does God Think About Me?* which explains God's actual heart for you as revealed in the Bible—God's written Word.

You Are Valuable

I am the Creator and you are my creation. I breathed into your nostrils the breath of life (Genesis 2:7). I created you in my own image (Genesis 1:27). My eyes saw your unformed substance (Psalm 139:16). I knit you together in your mother's womb (Psalm 139:13). I know the number of hairs on your head, and before a word is on your tongue, I know it (Matthew 10:30; Psalm 139:4). You are fearfully and wonderfully made (Psalm 139:14). You are more valuable than many sparrows (Matthew 10:31). I have given you dominion over all sheep and oxen and all beasts of the field and birds of the heavens and fish of the sea

(Psalm 8:6–8; Genesis 1:26, 28). I have crowned you with glory and honor as the pinnacle and final act of the six days of creation (Psalm 8:5; Genesis 1:26).

However, from the very beginning, you exchanged the truth about me for a lie. You worshiped and served created things rather than me, the Creator (Romans 1:25). You have sinned and fallen short of my glory (Romans 3:23). Just as I said to Adam and Eve, the penalty for your sin is death (Romans 6:23; Genesis 2:17). And in your sin, you were spiritually dead (Ephesians 2:1). You were children of wrath, living as enemies to me (Ephesians 2:3; Romans 5:10). You turned aside from me. You became corrupt. There is none who does good, not even one (Psalm 14:2–3). What you deserve is my righteous judgment (Psalm 7:11–12).

And yet, in my great love, I gave my unique Son, that all those who believe in him will not perish but have everlasting life (John 3:16). While you were still sinners, Christ died for you. While you were still hostile toward me, you were reconciled to me by the death of my Son (Romans 5:8, 10). Sin doesn't have the last word. Grace does (Romans 5:20).

Now everyone who calls on the name of Jesus will be saved (Romans 10:13). You who have believed are born-again (1 Peter 1:3). I have adopted you (Ephesians 1:5). You are children of God, heirs of God (1 John 3:2; Romans 8:16–17). You are no longer orphans. You belong to me (John 14:18; 1 Corinthians 6:19). And I love you as a perfect Father (1 John 3:1; Luke 15:20–24).

You Are New

In my eyes, [with your faith placed in my Son Jesus], you are a brand new creation. The old has passed away; the new has come (2 Corinthians 5:17). Sin is no longer your master, for you died to sin and are now alive to me (Romans 6:11; Ephesians 2:4–5).

You are finally free from the slavery of sin and death. There is now no condemnation for you (Romans 8:1–2). All your sins are forgiven (1 John 1:9). All your unrighteousness has been cleansed by the blood of Jesus (1 John 1:7, 9). You are now righteous in my sight with the very righteousness of my perfect Son (Romans 4:5).

You've been saved by grace (Ephesians 2:8). You've been justified by faith (Romans 5:1). You are utterly secure in me; nothing will be able to separate you from my love in Christ Jesus (Romans 8:39). No one is able to snatch you out of my hand (John 10:29). And I will never leave you nor forsake you (Hebrews 13:5).

You Have My Spirit

You not only have a new Father, but also a new family of brothers and sisters (Luke 8:21). You are now part of the people of God (1 Peter 2:9). And together the life you now live is by faith in my Son (Galatians 2:20).

Look to Jesus. Keep your eyes on him. He is the author and perfecter of your faith (Hebrews 12:2). Christ is in you by my Spirit, and you are in Christ (John 15:5; Colossians 1:27). Stay close to Jesus. Abide in him (John 15:4). For your life is found in him (John 14:6; Colossians 3:3–4). To live is Christ, and to die is gain (Philippians 1:21).

Don't live by your own power or understanding. No, live by my Spirit within you (Zechariah 4:6; Proverbs 3:5). Remember, I have given you the Holy Spirit to be with you and in you (Romans 5:5; John 14:17). The Spirit will guide you into all truth, help you to obey me, and empower you to do my work (John 16:7, 13; Acts 1:8; Galatians 5:16).

You Will Be Transformed

As you seek me and see more of my glory, I am transforming you into the image of my Son (2 Corinthians 3:18; Exodus 33:18). One day you will be changed, in a moment, in the twinkling of an eye, at the last trumpet sound (1 Corinthians 15:52). When Jesus appears, you will be like him, because you shall see him as he is (1 John 3:2; Romans 8:29).

You will be delivered from your body of death through Jesus Christ, and your dwelling place will be with me (Romans 7:24–25; John 14:3). And I will wipe away every tear from your eyes, and death shall be no more, neither shall there be mourning, nor crying, nor pain anymore (Revelation 21:3–4).

You will drink from the spring of the water of life without payment, and I myself will make for you a feast of rich food and well-aged wine (Revelation 21:6; Isaiah 25:6). You will enter my rest, inherit the Kingdom I've prepared for you, and step into fullness of joy and pleasures forevermore (Hebrews 4:9–11; Matthew 25:34; Psalm 16:11).

But most of all, you will see my face and be with me where I am (Revelation 22:4; John 14:3).

You Represent Me

Therefore, walk in a manner worthy of your calling (Ephesians 4:1). You are no longer darkness, but light in my Son. Walk as children of light (Ephesians 5:8). You are the light of the world, a city set on a hill (Matthew 5:14). I have called you (2 Peter 1:3). I have chosen you (Revelation 17:14). You are now a saint, a servant, a steward, and a soldier (Romans 1:7; Acts 26:16; 1 Peter 4:10; 2 Timothy 2:3). You are a witness and a worker (Acts 1:8; Ephesians 2:10). Through Jesus you are victorious (1 Corinthians 15:57). You have a glorious future (Romans 8:18). You are a citizen of heaven (Philippians 3:20). You are an ambassador for my Son (2 Corinthians 5:20).[1]

If you have come to place your faith in Jesus, then you *are* all these things and more to Almighty God, the Creator of all that exists, and the one true personal God. Understanding who we are in Christ is essential to our successfully living the abundant, victorious life Christ died to provide us. In John 10:10 we read Jesus saying "I came that they may have life and have it abundantly." The abundant life Christ offers is filled with new opportunities and responsibilities. In Christ, we can enjoy life abounding with fullness of joy and strength for mind, body, and soul. We can also enjoy a contrast to feelings of lack, emptiness, and dissatisfaction which motivate us to seek the true meaning of life and our place in God's plan. In 1 John 5:4-5 we read "For everyone who is born of God overcomes the world. And this is the victory that has overcome the world—our faith. Who is it that overcomes the world except the one who believes that Jesus is the Son of God?"

Contending for Your True Identity

The enemy of God continuously seeks ways to defeat us. The last thing he wants is for us to more fully discover who we are in Christ. Christ has already defeated the enemy, and the reality of the enemy's demise is *being* played out now. But so long as he can keep Christians deceived about the incredible authority and power they have in Christ, the less the enemy suffers, and more to his point, the less effective is God's plan. God's plan is to work in and through His people to transform the world. So, anything the enemy can do to prevent us from fully operating in Christ's authority and power, the less the world is transformed for good. The enemy's age-old tool is deception.

In the garden of Eden, the enemy enticed Eve to reconsider what God had said deceiving her about the reason for God's instruction. Appealing to their human curiosity, the enemy managed to get both Adam and Eve to doubt God's word and ultimately persuaded them to reject God.

The Bible refers to the enemy, Satan, as the "father of all lies." There is no truth in him. Yet, we listen to him and even believe his lies, which always causes us to needlessly suffer.

Understanding God's Grace

God's *grace* is a gift from Him that has been woefully misunderstood. I'm grateful to my pastor, Dr. Tom Barkey, for his years of study and instruction on the topic. We who come to believe in and receive Jesus by God's grace through faith, are called to impact the world. Ephesians 2:8 from the Amplified Bible reads: "For it is by free grace (God's unmerited favor) that you are saved (delivered from judgment and made partakers of Christ's salvation) through [your] faith. And this [salvation] is not of yourselves [of your own doing, it came not through your own striving], but it is the gift of God." Our salvation is a gift from God. God brings us to the point of realizing we need a Savior/Redeemer. Then, when we respond to Him, we are saved. By being saved, we are considered *justified* by faith. An easy to remember definition of the word *justified* is "It is just as if I never sinned." When a person chooses salvation through faith in Christ, all their sins—past, present and future—are removed from their account.

Grace is one way God demonstrates His tremendous love for us. But, grace is a word that has become misunderstood and therefore misapplied. The apostle Paul addressed this in chapters 5:20-6:2 of the book of Romans. Again, here I quote from the Amplified Classic:

> But then the Law came in, [only] to expand *and* increase the trespass [making it more apparent and exciting opposition]. But where sin increased *and* abounded, grace (God's unmerited favor) has surpassed it *and* increased the more *and* superabounded, so that, [just] as sin has reigned in death, [so] grace (His unearned and undeserved favor) might reign through righteousness (right standing with God) which issues in eternal life through Jesus Christ (the Messiah, the Anointed One) our Lord.
>
> What shall we say [to all this]? Are we to remain in sin in order that God's grace (favor and mercy) may multiply *and* overflow? Certainly not! How can we who died to sin, live in it any longer?[2]

The people to whom the apostle Paul wrote were attempting to distort and abuse God's grace. They reasoned they could *willfully practice* sin, and their sin would not be counted against them. Dietrich Bonhoeffer called this philosophy *Cheap Grace*, which is by continuing to sin cheapening the tremendous gift of grace God gives to us. By Jesus' death and resurrection, believers are forgiven of all sins, [sin is the rejection of God and all His instructions for life]. However, to willfully practice sinful behavior as a believer is presuming upon God's grace. To intentionally conduct oneself in ways known to be contrary to God's instruction is willful disobedience and is subject to the discipline of God.

To practice sin as a believer is a very serious matter. An unbeliever who sins is merely doing what comes naturally. But if you are truly *born again*, meaning by faith you have accepted Jesus as your personal Savior and Lord, when you sin, you will experience remorse. If you continue in your sinful behavior, you are positioning yourself to be disciplined by God. If you aren't experiencing remorse when you realize your sin, then you should question your salvation.

Defining *grace* as God's unmerited favor is an acceptable definition, but it's not quite complete. Additionally, God's grace is *His imparted ability for you to succeed in your transformation.* God wants us to succeed in being personally transformed to be collectively improving the world. The process of being transformed is also referred to as *sanctification.* This is the process by which we cooperate with God to have our soul (mind, will, emotions, and unique personality) transformed. As we study God's Word, as we fellowship with other believers, as we seek to grow in the knowledge and conviction of our faith, we are being *sanctified.*

If you have been a believer in Jesus for quite a while, but upon reflection, you can't see you have changed all that much, then you should question yourself. In which allures of this world are you still choosing to engage? If you are continuing to engage in sinful behaviors rather than choosing to cooperate with God, you are like the people to whom the apostle Paul wrote. And you are dangerously close to God removing the gift of grace from some area of your life. While the Bible makes clear that once a person places his or her faith in Jesus, their salvation is secured, our disobedience can bring God's discipline upon us in various ways, including God's removal of His grace upon an area of our life until we come back into right alignment.

The apostle Paul also wrote in Romans 1:21-32 that those who know God, but do not glorify Him as God, nor are thankful, and suppress the knowledge of God, are futile in their thoughts and foolish in their dark hearts and are, in effect, creating idols in place of God. Therefore, God gives them over to their sinful choices. God removes His gift of grace from those who willfully abuse it.

God's grace will increase in our lives the more we cooperate with His plan and purpose. I lived for many years as an unregenerate sinner, but from the moment I found Jesus and sensed my transformation, I rushed into God's arms. I wanted to get as far away from my former life as possible and as quickly as I could. I immersed myself in the Bible. I listened to Christian talk radio all day long every day. I found a church and immediately got involved in Bible study. I fell deeper and deeper in love with God and came to earnestly desire Him and His ways. I could see with greater clarity than ever that God is love, and all He desires for you and me is for us to be secure in His love. Christ died to ransom us from sin, thereby allowing to live an abundant, victorious life in Him. He desires that our transformation attracts others to the same saving knowledge of Jesus we've been graced to discover.

What It Means to Know God

Unique to Christianity, *knowing God* is a personal and experiential reality. The Old Testament Scriptures contain the oldest books of the Bible. God revealed Himself to His people in many ways, which you can learn about by reading the Old Testament.

What we learn in the book of Genesis, the first book of the Old Testament, is that we were created by God in His image to live in a vital, holy, loving relationship with Him and with one another. God's desire was and still is for us to be in a right relationship with Him. His desires with His love flowing in and through us, all who belong to God will be recognized by His love. But once sin entered the world through Adam and Eve, humanity was separated from God and all that was good. Nonetheless, God made the promise of sending a Redeemer, allowing those who wanted to be restored to a right relationship with God to experience restoration by faith.

The Old Testament was originally written in the Hebrew language. "To know" is the Hebrew word *yada*, a verb. Vine's Expository Dictionary of Biblical Words helps us understand the richness of the word *yada*.

> *Yada* means 1) to know by observing and reflecting (thinking), and 2) to know by experiencing. The first sense appears in Genesis 8:11 when Noah "knew" the waters had abated by seeing the freshly picked olive leaf in the dove's mouth; he "knew" it after observing and thinking about what he had seen. He did not actually see or experience the abatement [of the waters] himself.
>
> In contrast to knowing through reflection is the knowing which comes through experience with the senses, by investigation and proving, by reflection and consideration (firsthand knowing). Consequently, *yada* is used in synonymous parallelism with "hear, "see," and "perceive see."

[Yada] can represent that kind of knowing which one learns...or by being told. In this sense "know" is paralleled by "acknowledge" and "learn."

In addition to the essentially cognitive knowing already presented, this verb has a purely experiential side. The "knower" has actual involvement with or in the object of the knowing. Adam's knowing Eve also refers to direct contact with her—in a sexual relationship. In Gen. 18:19 God says He "knows" Abraham; He cared for him in the sense that He chose him from among the other men and saw to it that certain things happened to him. The emphasis is on the fact that God "knew" him intimately and personally. In fact, it is parallel in concept to "sanctified." A similar use of this word relates to God's relationship to Israel as a chosen or elect nation.

Yada in the intensive and causative stems is used to express a particular concept of revelation. God makes Himself known through revelatory acts ... [and] through the spoken word—for example, by the commands given to Moses ... Thus, God reveals Himself in law and promise.[3]

I love the word yada. Essentially, "to know" God is to have an abiding, intimate, experiential knowledge of Him. And God longs to know us the same way. The pure and beautiful loving relationship we can enjoy with God is the holiest love attainable—a love that comes from God to us, that we choose to receive and then choose to give back to Him.

Think about it: the love of God is what we were created to enjoy. Unless we are in right relationship with God through faith in Jesus by the power of the Holy Spirit, we cannot personally experience God's love.

Yet, in our estranged state, we benefit from God's love flowing through those who have placed their faith in Jesus. We can experience His love in a residual sense. But until and unless we choose to accept His offer of redemption, we will live outside of His perfect love—we will remain outside the family of God and His Fatherly love and benefit of His constant care.

J. I. Packer, Board of Governor's Professor of Theology at Regent College in Vancouver and author of the bestselling book *Knowing God* says, "What makes life worthwhile is having a big enough objective, something which catches our imagination and lays hold of our allegiance, and this the Christian has in a way that no other person has. For what higher, more exalted, and more compelling goal can there be than to *know God?*"[4]

God Created You with a Purpose in Mind

Everything, without exception, God does is intentional and with a purpose. In Pastor Rick Warren's bestselling book, *The Purpose Driven Life,* he reveals that we are each created by God with five purposes in mind:

- **We were planned for God's pleasure**

    so your first purpose is to offer real worship.

- **We were formed for God's family**

    so your second purpose is to enjoy real fellowship.

- **We were created to become like Christ,**

    so your third purpose is to learn real discipleship.

- **We were shaped for serving God**

    so your fourth purpose is to practice real ministry.

- **We were made for a mission**

    so your fifth purpose is to live out real evangelism.

Only when a person realizes the truth about their existence as created by God will they discover hope. When they actually embrace and live according to their created purpose, then they find true personal fulfillment. Moreover, by living out their God-created purpose, they become part of a reformation and movement by God for the benefit of many.

The Bible makes clear God is no respecter of persons. Each of us is equal in His eyes. With this realization firmly understood, the heavens are our limit. What we see God do in another person's life is possible for us. Granted, we are each unique, and we are each created with our own purpose in life on earth. God will always do for you that which will help you be His intended best—unique to you.

To the Old Testament prophet, Jeremiah, God said: "Before I formed you in the womb I *knew* you, and before you were born, I consecrated you; I appointed you a prophet to the nations" (Jeremiah 1:5, emphasis added). Just as God knew (yada) Jeremiah before he was conceived and had a plan and purpose for Jeremiah's life, He knows and plans for each of us. God's knowledge of us is complete and eternal. His love for us is eternal. His desires for us are ever and only for our good. He desires we live according to our created purpose so we can be an effective part of His plan to bring all who belong to Him into His family.

Ephesians 2:10 reads: "For we are his workmanship, created in Christ Jesus for good works, which God prepared beforehand, that we should walk in them."

Let's unpack Ephesians 2:10 so you can really embrace this truth for all it's worth.

We are His workmanship: This verse is unique and remarkable. It speaks of God's election and predestination, making us what we are. It also applies not only to our moment of salvation but to all good works that follow—we belong to Him, and therefore we are His responsibility. Once we place our faith in Christ, we are set wholly in the Father's care. The word translated "workmanship" (*poiema*) means that which has been made or is the result of someone's work. Poiema is where we get the English word poem. The noun occurs only twice in the New Testament and in both instances it is used of God's creative activity. In Romans 1:20 it is rendered "the things that are made" (ASV) and refers to the material creation. This world is not the result of a chance evolutionary process; it is the direct result of the creative work of the Eternal God. We can deduce then, that being His and His workmanship is extended to include first our creation—when we were naturally conceived.

Created in Christ Jesus: This creation, distinctively refers to the "new creation" we become the moment we place our faith in Jesus. First created in our natural state, then recreated through faith in Christ—in both, we are God's creatures. However, in our recreated state, we are uniquely able to commune with God and respond to His will for our lives.

For good works: Other translations state, "unto works of service." What is being conveyed here is God had a specific role for you to play in this world, to help usher in His kingdom, when all evil will ultimately be destroyed—when good will overcome evil. And with that role in mind, He created you. You are designed in such a way you can accomplish His specific plan or calling or assignment for you.

Which God prepared beforehand, that we should walk in them: God personally created you with a very specific purpose—a purpose for good, with the power and ability through faith in Christ to literally change the world. When we cooperate with God and walk out our lives according to His plan and purpose, only then can we experience true personal fulfillment. Think: when anything is utilized inconsistent with its design, optimal results are not obtained.

Willingly Partnering with God

Sadly, many people who come to a personal, saving knowledge of Jesus, continue to live out their lives as they please—they do not cooperate with God in the process of sanctification. The result is we have large numbers of people who profess to be Christians, but whose lives fail to demonstrate the love, authority, and power of God. This reality is sad for at least two reasons: 1.) the individuals themselves are missing out on enjoying a powerfully victorious and abundant life here and now; 2.) the world that needs to see the difference Jesus makes in people's lives is being dissuaded from the hope of the Christian faith.

Barna Research Group, a demographic research team, surveys professing Christians on a variety of topics. With a twenty-question survey, the Barna Research Group sought to learn the distinctions among self-professing Christians specific to their actually living the faith they profess. The summary of their findings was:

> Just over half of the nation's Christians—using the broadest definition of those who call themselves Christians—qualify for this category (51 percent). They tend to have attitudes and actions that are characterized by self-righteousness.
>
> On the other end of the spectrum, 14 percent of today's self-identified Christians—just one out of every seven— seem to represent the actions and attitudes consistent with those of Jesus.
>
> Additionally, 84 percent of young non-Christians say they know a Christian personally, yet only 15 percent say the lifestyles of the believers they know are noticeably different in a good way.[5]

I am on a mission to change this. I want people to understand the difference between being a genuine believer and being a genuinely effective believer. I am among the Christian believers who earnestly seek to be transformed daily because I'm convinced God's ways are far superior to anything the world can offer. I have experienced the amazing and wonderful blessings of being a Christian many times over in my life. I have hope and joy and peace and freedom not otherwise available. I have the confidence of God's love and value, so I aim high. I know the Holy Spirit lives within me, enabling me to do what I cannot do on my own. I am living my life consistent with my created purpose, so I have personal fulfillment. I see evidence of God at work in and through me that brings me joy and benefit others.

If you are a professing Christian who has not allowed God to transform you into the person He intended you to be before you were ever conceived, you are living in an unnecessary struggle between your new spirit and your old. No one can transition into something new, without letting go of the old.

Living an authentic Christian life is what the world needs like never before. When more people realize the reformation the world needs is possible with authentic Christ followers, then hope will flow. You can count on me to be among those who are positively making a difference in this world by our Christian influence. May I count on you?

In the next chapter, we'll explore the extravagant way God has provided for you.

CHAPTER SEVEN

God's Provision for You

There are so many benefits to being a child of God, beginning with the transformation from being a sinner entirely estranged *from* God to a saint who is wholly related *to* God. I know the transformation seems too good to be true, but it *is* true because of all God has done, motivated by His love for you.

When a person chooses to be in a right relationship with God through faith in Jesus, the Holy Spirit supernaturally transforms their dead, natural-born spirit to an entirely new, living, supernaturally born spirit—you become an entirely new creature—one who never before existed. This instant transformation is *salvation*. You are *saved* from the debt of sin and instantly placed in a new position in relationship with God.

Once saved, you are *justified*. Justification is a gift from God, a reward for choosing to believe Him for His Word—that is, His Word fulfilled in the person of Jesus. Justification is more than a reset, but rather is a whole new spirit and an entirely new start. Not a single sin—past, present or future—will be a cause for God to judge you. Jesus paid for *all* of them. His life, death, and resurrection paid the entire debt of sin for the entire number of those who *repent* and place their faith in Jesus. Repent means to completely turn in the opposition direction. To repent is to change your mental and spiritual attitude from sin (rejection of God) and toward embracing God and His ways. Repentance turns you from the path toward hell onto the path to heaven.

Those who chose to repent of their natural-born, sinful self and enter into God's love by faith in Christ are recognized by God as *righteous*—that is, they are deemed by God to be morally right, justified, and virtuous. No matter what kind of life you have lived, no matter what immoral and harmful things you've done, you are not condemned by those any longer— no one is ever denied restoration with God through a genuine faith in Jesus. Romans 8:1 says "There is therefore now no condemnation for those who are in Christ Jesus." But, salvation is just the beginning of the many benefits of belonging to God.

Once you have been saved and justified, then you enter into the next part of the process known as *sanctification*, which was discussed some in chapter six. To be *sanctified* is to willingly cooperate with the process of the Holy Spirit to become educated in order to operate according to the new life you now have in Christ. Through faith in Christ, a person is entirely transformed from an enemy of God to a full-fledged member of His family, a joint heir with Jesus. You have literally been transformed from abject poverty into a part of the royal priesthood and family of God. Amazing!

A Cooperative Effort

As with any relationship, our relationship with God is a cooperative endeavor. We each have a part in building, nurturing, and protecting the relationship. Growing in a relationship and in the process of sanctification requires cooperation on our part.

As stated before, human beings are made in three parts. However, it is the soul that is the connector of our body to our spirit, and for that reason, we need to consider the soul further. Dr. Grant Mullen explains:

> Our soul … is our personality which includes our mind, will, and emotions. It is the part of us that relates to other humans. It is shaped by all of our accumulated life experiences. I like to think of it as being attached to a huge bag or drag net into which all our life events go. These experiences both good and bad, shape our personalities and determine how we relate to others.
>
> Thought and emotion are the only parts of us that exist in both the natural and spiritual worlds. Wholeness in this part of our being will always require healing in both the natural and spiritual aspects of thought and emotion. One cannot come to complete emotional wholeness if treatment is directed at only the natural or spiritual aspect of man. God wants to bring us to freedom in both realms.[1]

Our spirit is made new at salvation. However, our souls and bodies remain the same unless we cooperate with the Holy Spirit to have our soul and body come into alignment with our new spirit. Our thoughts and emotions, part of our soul, have suffered and been wounded at some level simply by living in this world with all its evil. God wants to make us whole, healthy and free from the ravages of sin. Therefore, the apostle Paul wrote, "Do not be conformed to this world, but be transformed by the renewal of your mind, that by testing you may discern what is the will of God, what is good and acceptable and perfect" (Romans 12:2). Our thought life and our emotional being need to be transformed to enjoy the full benefits of being a child of God. Because our thought life and our emotional being remain subjected to the natural world even as a new Christian, healing in these two areas of our soul require both natural and a spiritual treatment. Again, referring to Dr. Grant Mullen:

> Before salvation, we are outside God's Kingdom and in the domain of Satan. There he molds us into his image by wounding us in as many ways as possible. These accumulated wounds leave deep scars in our personalities which cause lifelong emotional bondage. The longer we live in Satan's kingdom, the greater will be our accumulated wounds and personality damage.
>
> When we become Christians, our spirit immediately transfers ownership to God as we enter His kingdom. From this point on, we begin to have a relationship with God as He fills our spirit with His own. The Holy Spirit then begins the process of transforming us into God's image.
>
> When we enter God's kingdom our body doesn't usually change much. If we wore glasses before salvation, we usually wear them afterwards. Once in the kingdom however, we are given the privilege of praying for divine healing. The body is still subject to the consequences of the Fall, [original sin of Adam and Eve] which means it is still subject to disease and malfunction. The eventual transformation of our physical bodies will take place in heaven. Until then, we have to cope with somewhat unreliable physical containers for our eternal spirits.
>
> What happens to our soul or personality at the moment of salvation? One way of looking at this question is to consider another one. How much must we change to

qualify to become Christians? Well obviously we don't have to change at all. God, through the miracle of His grace takes us just the way we are so that He can clean us up and transform us into His image. "But God demonstrates His own love for us in this: While we were still sinners, Christ died for us." Romans 5:8 This means of course that we enter the kingdom in a sorry state, broken, bleeding, wounded with deeply damaged personalities from all the years that we have spent in Satan's kingdom. God accepts us as we are, damaged goods, "factory seconds."

It is possible then, to be a new Christian and still be bound in sinful habits and attitudes, with dysfunctional relationships, deep personality scars, addictions and compulsions. In other words, a new Christian can still have a very active and contaminated old nature which wreaks havoc in their mind even though their spirit now belongs to God.[2]

Before our salvation, our old nature accumulated pain and scars Satan imposed on us to mold us into his image. After salvation, we still have our old nature that will continue to adversely impact us—unless we cooperate with the Holy Spirit's transforming process.

Because our thought life and our emotional being both operate in the *mind*, healing of our thoughts and emotions must be addressed in the mind. If we allow our mind to stay the same as old nature, then our thoughts, our emotions, and our body will continue to suffer. However, if we cooperate with the Holy Spirit to allow our minds to be renewed consistent with the will of God, then we can find health, gain freedom, and have our soul transformed.

The battle is for the mind. Satan desperately wants to influence and control your thoughts by keeping your old nature alive and your new nature suppressed. God wants to set you free from your old nature so your mind will be free to think His thoughts and lead you out of the bondage of your past and into your new nature and destiny in Christ.

Embracing the Holy Spirit

The Holy Spirit is a distinct personal being with definite characteristics. He is not an impersonal force or an emanation of the power of God. The Holy Spirit is one Person of the Triune Godhead. He is equal to the Father, who is equal to the Son, who is equal to the Holy Spirit. Each Person of the Trinity is equal in nature but distinct in role and relationship. The distinct roles typically have the Father willing, the Son accomplishing, and the Spirit applying the work of the Son. The Holy Spirit's work always glorifies Christ Jesus.

The Holy Spirit's role in Jesus' human life is often unappreciated. The Spirit brought about the incarnation (Luke 1:35), anointed Jesus for His earthly ministry at His baptism, (Matthew 3:16; Mark 1:10; Luke 3:21-22), filled Jesus with the Holy Spirit (Luke 4:1), led and empowered Jesus (Luke 4:14, 18) and raised Jesus from the dead (Romans 8:11).

In our lives, the Spirit plays a prominent role beginning with the *atoning* work of Christ (meaning the debt of sin Christ paid to reconcile believers unto God). The atonement is a Trinitarian accomplishment, with the Holy Spirit playing a prominent role. Hebrews 9:14 states "how much more will the blood of *Christ*, who through the eternal *Spirit* offered Himself without blemish to *God*, purify our conscience from dead works to serve the living *God*"(emphasis added). All three Persons of the Godhead are included in

Hebrews 9:14, revealing atonement is accomplished for us by the totality of God.

In Scripture, the Holy Spirit is given many names to reveal that He, like the Father and the Son, is personal in nature. Descriptive names such as, Comforter, Helper, and Teacher reveal ways in which the Holy Spirit applies the accomplishments of Jesus for us. The Holy Spirit's work is central in the promises of the new covenant. The Spirit is the primary Person of the Trinity at work in applying the finished work of Christ to the lives of God's people. The power of the Spirit is the catalyst for spiritual transformation.

> Prayer, church attendance, moral living, coming from a Christian family, and knowing all the right religious words are not a sufficient basis for assurance of one's salvation. But one clear guarantee that someone has passed from death into life is the Spirit's work transforming that person's manner of living. He marks the life and character of believers in a definitive way.[3]

Scripture reveals the moment a person confesses faith in Jesus, the Holy Spirit is given to indwell the believer as a guarantee of their newly regenerated spirit (2 Corinthians 1:22; 5:5 and; Ephesians1:14). The Holy Spirit is resident within us ever at ready to enable us to live our new lives in Christ.

Evidence the Holy Spirit is at work in us is referred to as *fruit, or the fruit of the Spirit*. The fruit of the Holy Spirit is love, joy, peace, patience, kindness, goodness, faithfulness, gentleness, and self-control. When these are evident in our lives, we have proof the Holy Spirit has been allowed to transform us. I say *allowed* because as previously stated, transformation is a cooperative process. A believer can choose to cooperate or not.

Spiritual Offices and Gifts

There is controversy among Christians about whether the spiritual gifts operate today. I discussed this in some detail in *Renew Your Hope! Remedy for Personal Breakthroughs*. My simple response here, however, is since the Bible clearly states the end times for creation will be exceedingly difficult with evil advancing like never before, that God would leave us with less ability to overcome evil than He did the early church makes no sense at all. In the New Testament, we read of a great many miraculous events and displays of spiritual gifts imparted through many, not just the early *apostles*. (Apostle was the title given to the first twelve disciples of Christ as well as Paul and Barnabas.) There is controversy among Christians whether the office of an apostle exists today … Christians are people with differing opinions. However, if Christians were of the mindset to unite on what we agree upon and to leave what we don't agree upon up to the Holy Spirit to resolve, we'd make a better impression on the world.

I've experienced spiritual gifts of all sorts because I believe they exist. Jesus was unable to perform miracles in His own hometown because of the unbelief of the people—the Spirit would be wasting His powerful displays among those who refuse to believe. When Jesus was before the Jewish leaders and had already performed many signs and wonders, the leaders asked Him to display a miracle. He replied, "'An evil and adulterous generation seeks for a sign, but no sign will be given to it except the sign of Jonah.' So he left them and departed" (Matthew 16:4).

I've yet to meet a person who claims they do not believe in miracles for today, but who wouldn't readily embrace one if the miracle changed their life for the better.

Scripture reveals the Holy Spirit assigns spiritual offices:

- Apostles—a messenger, one sent forth with orders, the first in the Christian church to initiate and direct the preaching of the *gospel* (the good news of Jesus).

- Prophets—one who equips the *saints* (believers) for works of service through exhortation, edification, and consolation.

- Evangelists—one who devotes him/herself to preaching the gospel.

- Pastors—one who is gifted to lead, guide and set an example for Christians under their care.

- Teachers—one who devotes his or her life to preaching and teaching the Christian faith.

Scripture also reveals the Holy Spirit gives believers spiritual gifts such as:

- Prophecy—the ability to speak forth, proclaim and declare the divine will, to interpret the purposes of God, or to make known in a way the truth of God which is designed to influence people.

- Helps/Serving—ability to aid or render assistance to others in the church, ministering with compassion and grace, encompassing a broad range of applications, often consistent with one's talents.

- Teaching—the gift of effectively communicating truths of the Bible to others.

- Exhortation—the ability to motivate Christians to patient endurance, brotherly love, and good works.

- Giving—contributing to the needs of others as an agent of God's grace and mercy.

- Leadership/Administration—one who is set over others or who presides or rules or who attends with diligence and care to a matter.

- Mercy—ability to be compassionate in attitudes, words and actions; love enacted with the heart to meet the immediate needs of others and alleviate suffering, loneliness, and grief.

- Word of Wisdom—the ability to understand and speak forth biblical truth in such a way as to skillfully apply it to life situations with all discernment.

- Word of Knowledge—the gift of knowledge to understand the deep things of God and the mysteries of His Word.

- Faith—extraordinary confidence in God's promises, power, and presence, expressed by taking heroic stands for the expected God-intended/God-revealed outcome.

- Gifts of Healings—the supernatural manifestation of the Spirit of God that miraculously brings healing and deliverance from disease and/or infirmity.

- Miracles—the power to do supernatural works with the goal of furthering the kingdom of God, in a broad spectrum of ways. Casting out demons and raising from the dead are just two examples.

- Distinguishing between spirits—the ability to distinguish between the truth of the Word and the deceptive doctrines propagated by demons; and to discern, distinguish, or to discriminate the source of a spiritual manifestation—whether it emanates from a good or evil spirit.

- Tongues—ability to speak in a language a person does not know to minister to someone who does speak that language. Additionally, the ability to speak or sing a heavenly prayer language that is not one's native or learned tongue.

- Interpretation of Tongues—the ability to hear an utterance given in tongues (a language the person does not know) and provide the interpretation to impart understanding.

The endless love of God is expressed through each person of the Godhead. The one Person many fail to properly relate to is the Holy Spirit. My prayer is you embrace Him because He is the very power inside you who raised Jesus from the dead. He is the very power who fortifies believers everywhere to step into their God-given destiny and change the world for the better.

God's Love Seeks Our Best

There are many benefits to being rightly related to God. As an example, just using one Bible chapter—Psalm 103—note the many benefits we can glean:

A. Spiritually (v. 3, 12)

Spiritually, God's love removes the barrier that separates us from Him by canceling the debt of our sin so we can enjoy a loving relationship with Him. God's love removes our sins as though they never existed.

B. Emotionally (v. 3)

Much of our physical and emotional illness is due to moral failure. In removing the sin and guilt from our lives, God's love brings healing to our emotional life.

C. Eternally (v. 4)

The pit is the pit of death. God's love rescues us, fallen humanity, from our own bent on destruction and grants us eternal life.

D. Authoritatively (v. 4)

God's love places a crown of royal glory and authority on us. God's love "… made us a kingdom, priests to His God and Father" (Rev. 1:6). We have been crowned with His love and given a new citizenship on this earth and in heaven.

E. Physically (v. 5)

Like a father He desires to give us good gifts of strength and endurance. Jesus, the embodiment of God's love came enjoying life, and He wants His children to do the same.

F. Judicially (v. 6)

Here we find a major difference between divine love and what so often passes for love among people. Often, love is expressed as that virtue that accepts everything. But, God's love always makes judgment calls. Divine love hates what is wrong and embraces what is right.[4]

A person can become a Christian and never cooperate with the Holy Spirit to have their mind renewed and transformed. This is often due to ignorance because the person is trying to live in both their old and new natures. When we remain outside God's will as believers, for any reason, we subject ourselves to His discipline. He loves us too much to leave us in our disobedient state. So, if you feel the nudging of the Lord to do something different, take heed. His loving correction is always easier to take than His rod of discipline.

God's Many Provisions

Besides the utter demonstration of His love for you in the earthly life of Jesus and the indwelling of the Holy Spirit, God provides us a great deal more. Here are some additional provisions, although as you embrace your Christian life, you will discover more.

Ministering Angels

Angels are spiritual beings created by God to serve Him, though created higher than man (see Psalm 8:5 and Hebrews 2:7). However, according to 1 Corinthians 6:3, Christians, with Christ, will judge with Christ the angels and matters pertaining to this life. Some of the angels God created rebelled against God and were cast out of heaven. To this day, they continue to stand in active opposition to the work and plan of God. Others have remained obedient to Him and carry out His will. Angels are servants of God and described by the author of Hebrews as ministering spirits sent out to render service for the sake of those who will inherit salvation. (See Hebrews 1:14. See also Psalm 91:11 and Matthew 4:11).

Many times in Scripture, we read where God dispatched angels to assist humans. Often, in response, humans fall on their knees in awe, but the angel is quick to instruct the person not to worship him. Only God is worthy of our praise and worship by both man and angels.

In His sovereign wisdom, God does not always send angels to intervene. In His wondrous plan, God sometimes uses suffering, (a tool of growth, to manifest the character of Christ, to witness to others, etc.)

The Bible has much to say about angels:

- Angels are not divine and are not to be worshiped (Psalm 103:20; Revelation. 19:10; 22:9).
- As a separate order of creatures, they are both distinct from human beings and higher than humans with powers far beyond our abilities in this present age (Psalm 8:5; 1 Corinthians. 6:3; Hebrews. 1:14; Revelation 18:1).

- But, as creatures, they are limited in their powers, knowledge, and activities (Psalm 103:20; Mark 13:32; 1 Peter 1:11-12; 2 Peter 2:11; Revelation 7:1; Revelation 12:7).

- Like all of creation, angels are under God's authority and subject to His judgment (Matthew. 25:41;1 Corinthians. 6:3).

Angels Praise and Worship—Psalm 103:20, Luke 2:13-14, and Revelation 5:11-12 reveal that angels worship God day and night, proclaiming His awesome goodness.

Angels Protect—While there is no passage in Scripture that states each of us has an assigned "guardian angel," we read in Psalm 91:11 that angels do guard or protect us. Angels commissioned by God care for us, protect us from physical harm, and do battles with spiritual powers in the heavenly places that impact us here on Earth.

Angels Minister—God sends angels to minister to those who hurt or need strength. In the Garden of Gethsemane Jesus prayed and wrestle with what was to come. Luke 22:43 states that an angel appeared from heaven, "strengthening him." After Jesus had spent forty days in the wilderness resisting the temptations of the devil, Matthew 4:11 reveals "Then the devil left Him" ... "angels came and were ministering to Him." That they are ministering spirits who minister to the saints is presented as a general truth of the Bible.

Angels have Rank and Orders—The Bible reveals ranks among angels and specific orders or assignments as well. Michael the Archangel, for example, is particularly involved in ministry to Israel.

Angels Provide—When Elijah needed to be fed, angels brought food to him (1 Kings 19:5-6). When Jesus finished His forty days in the wilderness, angels were sent by God to provide sustenance (Matthew 4:11).

Angels Proclaim God's Truth—Angels are messengers by the very meaning of the word *angel*. They announced the birth of John the Baptist and of Jesus. Throughout the Bible, angels are reported as being involved in communicating God's truth or message.

Angels Punish or Carry Out God's Judgments—Angels are empowered to do anything God orders them to do. The book of Revelation indicates that angels, good and evil, will be at war in the end times with the good winning the last battle in God's plan to rid creation of all manner of sin and wickedness.

However, caution is warranted to properly discern if an angel is from God or not.

1. Angels will never minister in a manner that contradicts the Bible.

2. The actions of holy angels will always be consistent with the character of Christ.

3. Holy angels will always and only glorify God.

4. Angels are servants of God, just as we are servants of God. Don't be misled and hold them in high esteem. Only evil angels desire to be esteemed.

5. Scripture does not teach us to call upon angels. We're to pray to God, and He will dispatch angels according to His will.

6. Know what the Bible teaches, so you will not be deceived by fallen angels.

The Bible

As the written Word of God, the Bible is one of the most precious gifts He's given us. Today's Bible has been confirmed with objective, verifiable evidence to be the same today as the earliest known manuscript. Clearly, God watches over His Word not only to perform according to what He's said (Jeremiah 1:12) but to protect His Word. If all we had was an oral account of what God wanted to communicate to us, we would have no way to objectively confirm the truth of what was said. I love that God has provided us His Word in written form, so we can pore over the words again and again and be reminded that God's Word is unchangeable, because He Himself is unchangeable. What a precious provision for our faith.

Fellowship and Community

Another valuable provision from God is fellowship with the community of fellow believers. In chapter two, I discussed the innate desire of humanity to belong. We are created to function in community with one another. The beauty of this for believers is we can encourage one another in the faith. God even warns us not to forget the assembling of the saints. Hebrews 10:24-25 states: "And let us consider how to stir up one another to love and good works, not neglecting to meet together, as is the habit of some, but encouraging one another, and all the more as you see the Day drawing near."

I love a story attributed to Dr. John MacArthur, that tells of a member of a church, a young man who had regularly been attending, and who had stopped going. Noticing this, his pastor decided to visit him. The evening happened to be chilly, so the young man invited the pastor in to sit near the fireplace. After a long and awkward period of silence, the pastor took the fire tongs and carefully picked up a brightly burning ember and placed it to one side of the hearth away from the fire. Then he sat back in the comfortable chair. The room remained silent except for the crackling and sizzling of the fire.

After a longer period, the ember that had been set aside asserted a momentary glow, then its fire was gone. The young man observed everything with fascination. More time elapsed and by now, what had been a vibrant ember was cold and lifeless.

Not a word had been spoken since the initial greeting. The pastor finally stood up, picked up the cold, dead ember, and placed it back in the middle of the fire. Immediately it began to catch fire and glow with the light and warmth of the burning wood around it.

As the pastor reached the door to leave, the young man said, "Thank you, Pastor, for your visit and especially the fiery sermon. You'll see me back in church next Sunday."

Fellowship and community are part of God's design to keep us burning brightly and hot so we won't grow cold and dead. Church attendance is not a duty, but rather nourishment to our new spirit and encouragement to persevere unto the fullness of God's promises.

Dreams, Visions, and the Still Small Voice

There are many ways God provides for us. He will occasionally communicate with us through dreams. I have had a few night dreams that seemed very clearly to indicate God was guiding and protecting me. One dream, in particular, was disturbing. I dreamed about unfaithfulness. I woke quite perplexed. I prayed about the dream, seeking God's wisdom and counsel. I soon understood He was warning me about an investment I'd made without praying to Him first for guidance. I'd put seven-thousand dollars down on a venture that was supposed to help me discover new ways of making income online. After contemplating my decision before the Lord, I realized He was warning me this investment would not produce fruit because I had not been faithful to seek His direction before committing. We certainly couldn't afford to lose seven-thousand dollars, and I didn't want to be unfaithful to God.

Gratefully, because of God's love, He warned me in time to cancel my contract, according to the terms of the agreement. The company tried to strong arm, even threaten me, but I had the terms in black and white, and I was within the time frame to cancel and get a full refund. I got my money back and, in all repentance, thanked the Lord for His amazing provision.

In the next chapter, we'll explore how you can learn more about your God-given talents and spiritual gifts and in so doing, realize your personal purpose in life.

CHAPTER EIGHT

God's Invitation to You

Hopefully, at this point, you've begun to embrace the truth about who God says you are. Restating what was written in chapter four, God only made one of you. You are unique. There is none other like you. You are uniquely valuable to God. Your value and significance to God are tremendous because you are one of a kind. Your name is written on the palms of His hands (Isaiah 49:16). God wants you to know Him and to know He is love, so much so, *He personally lived the human existence, suffered, and died for you.*

Believe and Receive

I asked you to consider placing your faith in Jesus in chapter four. Perhaps you weren't ready then. I sincerely hope as you've read further and gained more understanding, you are ready to embrace God and enter into a transformed life of freedom, joy, and victory over all evil. With your faith placed in Jesus as your personal Savior and Lord, you are in a position to embrace your God-intended purpose in life and live in such a way that you make a tremendous difference in this world.

All God offers and wants us to have is an utterly amazing reality. Not only can we be restored into a right relationship with God and experience His lavish love, but we can know our true purpose in life and partner with God to have His kingdom established on earth. This is the reformation the world needs. God's plan is for us to be saved by Him so He can then work through us to save many more. We are saved to serve. And when we comprehend this and join in an effort far bigger than ourselves, not only are we fulfilled, but we are fulfilling what is known as The Great Commission.

C. S. Lewis as quoted earlier in this book said, "If I find in myself a desire which no experience in this world can satisfy, then the most probable explanation is that I was made for another world."[1] For those who have placed their faith in Christ, nothing of this world can truly satisfy. We are now united with God and have the privilege of joining Him in fulfilling His plan.

Jesus appeared in His risen state to the eleven remaining apostles and spoke to them saying, "All authority in heaven and on earth has been given to me. Go therefore and make disciples of all nations, baptizing them in the name of the Father and of the Son and of the Holy Spirit, teaching them to observe all that I have commanded you. And behold, I am with you always, to the end of the age" (Matthew 28:18-20).

Those who embrace God's love and then devote their life to His plan are the reformers the world needs. Imagine the impact on the world if great numbers of people discovered God's love, gave their life to Christ, and then lived out their faith! Together we *will* push back the wickedness, corruption, and evil in our world. If this is a reformation you want to be a part of, then make sure to start by choosing to believe in and receive Jesus as God's promised Redeemer. Choose today to repent from your current life and to embrace the transformed life Christ offers you.

If you realize you have been living according to your will instead of God's will, and you want to enjoy the fullness of His promises, now is the time to do so without delay.

Right now, declare with your voice you want to be restored to God the Father, and you choose to place your faith in Jesus as your personal Savior and Lord. State you are turning from your former ways, and now embrace God's ways. Thank God for His Holy Spirit who indwells every believer the moment they place their faith in Christ.

And now, rejoice! All the hosts in heaven are rejoicing over you. Jesus said, "Just so, I tell you, there will be more joy in heaven over one sinner who repents than over ninety-nine righteous persons who need no repentance" (Luke 15:7).

Fortifying Your Faith

One of the first things we must do as a new believer, a Christian, is to connect with fellow believers. As illustrated by the story of the pastor who visited the absentee church member in the previous chapter, we are all part of the same fire. We need to stay connected to produce the greatest good and to prevent any part of the community from becoming cold and dead, extinguishing their effectiveness for the kingdom.

If there are people in your life whom you respect, who have been living a demonstrated life of faith in Jesus, share with them your new commitment to Christ. Ask them to help you get connected with other believers so you can grow in your faith. If you don't have anyone in your life who can be a mentor, then your first step is to find one if possible. Check with people you know and respect to learn if they can help you network to find a Christian mentor or a local church.

All Churches are Not Equal

Knowing what to look for in a church is essential. Unfortunately, there are many doctrines and denominations—some are worthy, and some are not. Following is a list of things you want to make sure the church you choose to attend embraces.

- Believes in the authority and inerrancy of the Bible
- Has no other book of religious authority than the Bible
- Teaches salvation comes by faith in Jesus alone (no other act needed)
- Centers on the gospel of Jesus Christ
- Holds to sound biblical doctrine (that which is taught)
- Preaches expositionally (providing explanation and application)
- Teaches the Bible
- Enjoys biblical and God-centered worship
- Has biblically qualified and mutually accountable leadership
- Employs leaders and pastors who are nurturing to their people
- Encourages people to pray
- Encourages people to study the Bible
- Encourages and equips people to grow in discipleship
- Equips people to serve God
- Maintains a culture of grace, love, and peace
- Offers ample opportunity for fellowship
- Emphasizes evangelistic in nature and outreach

You will likely have other things you want to look for in a church. The style of music, the service times, childcare and/or children's classes, active group for your age range, etc. These are legitimate matters, but the list above should be first and foremost to make certain you are participating in a church that will not lead you astray.

One organization many trustworthy ministries rely upon to help people find a local church is Church Angel. By going to their website, www.churchangel.com, you can enter specific criteria, and they will recommend a variety of churches.

Personal Accountability

Having a mentor in the Christian faith is always a good idea. Seek to find someone whom you trust, who would be willing to meet with you on a regular or semi-regular basis. This could be a person who is already teaching a Bible study group you can join, or simply a mature believer with whom you have a good relationship. I've learned when seeking a mentor, you need to be specific about what you'd like. For example:

- Frequency of contact
- Where/how to connect
- The length of time for each meeting
- The length of time for the mentoring
- Mutual transparency

Establishing the duration for the mentoring helps all involved to not feel burdened. A length of six months is a good way to start. If both parties desire, the mentoring can continue after the first time period is complete. Again, it's advisable to agree on a time limit than to leave the arrangement open-ended.

Mentoring is also available through books, Christian radio and television, Christian interest groups, seminars, etc. Just be certain the same criteria for selecting a church exists with any individual or program you seek to learn from.

Bible Study

Getting involved in Bible study is essential. If your new-found church has a Bible study program that fits you, great. If not, again use the church criteria for finding a good Bible study.

I had the privilege of teaching for Community Bible Study (CBS) for several years. CBS is international, interdenominational, and independent of any church. As I personally know the statement of faith and the methods of operation, I can highly recommend this organization. CBS can be found online at http://www.communitybiblestudy.org/. They have classes for men, women, children, and youth. Their various studies are available in about fifty different languages and for many different types of groups. In the United States, there are classes offered in languages other than English, classes for mildly intellectually impaired adults, and discussion and socialization groups for young adults to meet the unique needs of the millennial generation. Many classes also offer infant and toddler care. Visit the website for CBS to learn about classes local to you.

Finding Your Place in God's Plan

One of the things that interferes with people finding their place in God's plan is the incorrect idea that what God will want from them will be absolutely horrible and will interfere with the things they want to do.

Do you think that God, who is love, and who wants nothing but what's in our best interest, would demand something of us that was less than loving or in our best interest? The idea that serving God will be entirely disagreeable is a lie from the enemy.

Missionaries, who end up in some third-world country in a hut with a thatched roof and a dirt floor have the *passion* for going there to share God's Word. God created them with the passion and the specific talents, and He'll equip them with the spiritual gifts they need to do what He's asked them to do. Such missionaries love their work, with all its harsh realities, difficulties, and sacrifices. Additionally, the Holy Spirit goes with us wherever we are to lead and guide us.

God has created you with natural talents for you to use to further His kingdom on earth. Those things you are naturally gifted at and enjoy doing are what He wants you to use in His service. Certainly, there will be times when serving according to your God-given passion is difficult and somewhat sacrificial, but isn't that true of anything worth devotion? Being a parent or becoming a business owner is harsh, difficult, and sacrificial, yet look at the return on the investment. God always equips His people with what they need to accomplish the assignment He's given.

Beyond your natural talents and passion, God gives His people grace. Grace has always existed as part of the character of God, which is displayed by His gifts to men. God's grace was epitomized on the cross of Christ. God's grace is expressed in a wide variety of forms. Sustaining grace is grace God gives at special times of need, especially during adversity or suffering. God also gives us His favor so we can discover specific opportunities to serve. He gives us His anointing, which allows others to recognize we are sent by Him.

Consider your natural talents and abilities. What are you naturally good at and enjoy doing? When you identify natural talents and abilities that can be used to serve/benefit others, you've discovered keys to identifying your life's purpose. Which of the following talents/abilities do you have?

- Plumbing/Electrical
- Construction
- Carpentry
- Art
- Writing
- Music
- Singing
- Sewing/Crafts
- Administration
- Leadership
- Research
- Teaching
- Other:

- Dance
- Media
- Hospitality
- Cooking
- Custodial
- Organizational abilities
- Accounting
- Internet Technology
- Working with women
- Working with elderly
- Working with children
- Working with adults
- Caring for infants

These are just a few ideas. Even a skill such as driving your vehicle can be put into kingdom service. We are saved to serve (2 Timothy 1:9). We are not saved by service, but for service (Romans 7:4).

Your new church may have a formal program to help you discover your talents and then find a place within the church where you can use them. If not, find out what the procedures and requirements are for you to volunteer. All churches, everywhere, need more help. You will get the greatest blessing of all because you'll be operating according to your natural talents and abilities and making a kingdom difference.

About five years after embracing Jesus, after immersing myself in all things Christian, we moved to a new community where we had no family or friends. I had to find a new church, and I'd hoped there would be a

Community Bible Study class for me to attend. After a few visits to different churches, we found a church but no CBS. I called the organization's headquarters and learned I could help them start a new class. I'd already started a few businesses, so I agreed. After a while, I sensed the Lord leading me to be the class teacher. I had done some keynote presentations and such as a professional woman, but I'd never really taught. Certainly, I wasn't hearing God correctly. I'd only been a believer for a short time. There's no way I could teach. Some time went by, and I couldn't shake the impression I was to volunteer to teach. I told the Area Director, and we prayed. I took three days to consider how I would respond to God. Ultimately, I agreed to be the Teaching/Director for the class. This role would require I not only teach, but work as director for the class—identifying and training leadership according to the policies and procedures of CBS.

That decision turned out to be the very best decision of my life up to then. Teaching requires a ton of study and the ability to share complex matters in a simple and comprehensible manner. I didn't know, but I'm a natural teacher. From studying to teach, my own knowledge of my new-found faith was tremendously increased. I think I got more benefit than any of the class members by having the privilege to teach for what turned out to be nearly seven years.

Despite the many difficulties I encountered directing the leadership and teaching the class, my service was a most rewarding and fulfilling effort. Yes, there were many difficult situations my leadership team and I had to work through. But we did everything prayerfully seeking God's guidance. Together we successfully worked through all obstacles.

Discovering Your Spiritual Gifts

As discussed in chapter seven, your spiritual gift(s) are assigned to you by the Holy Spirit. Your new-found church may have a class or method to help you identify your spiritual gifts. Spiritual gifts are always for the benefit of the Church—that is, all believers.

If your church does not have a preferred spiritual gift evaluation method, you might consider the various spiritual gift tests available online. One web site I especially like is www.chazown.com. This site not only helps you identify your spiritual gifts, but also your passion, vision, and purpose. *Chazown* is the Hebrew word for vision or dream. This site helps you discover and pursue God's dream for your life. Two other websites I reviewed include GiftsTest.com and SpiritualGiftsTest.com. I encourage you to look around. Gift tests exist for general groups or specific groups such as men, women, teens, etc.

I am careful who and what I recommend for your sake and my own reputation. When you consider a spiritual gift evaluation resource, make sure their doctrine is sound by reading their statement of faith. From the two websites provided you can learn even more about spiritual gifts than I share in this book. You can also take a test to help identify what gift(s) the Holy Spirit has allocated to you.

Every believer has at least one spiritual gift. Once you discover yours, you'll need to be in a group or mentoring setting where you can safely begin to exercise your gift(s). You can ask your pastor to put you in touch with others mature in the faith and capable of helping you.

Remember, spiritual gifts are bestowed by the Holy Spirit for Him to work through you. You have done nothing to deserve the gift, so you have no cause to boast or be prideful. In fact, to do so, will position you to be disciplined by God. Humility and gratitude for the opportunity to serve the

One who gave His all for us should be the prevailing attitude of all believers. As I said every night signing off from my radio show, "Remember, Christ died for us. The least we can do is live for Him."

The Many Invitations from God

There are a great many invitations from God in Scripture beyond what I've shared in this chapter so far. Here are three invitations as identified and commented on by Billy Graham, a prominent American Christian evangelist, condensed as printed here. The following is used with permission:

The first invitation is an invitation to rest.

Jesus said, "Come to Me, all you who labor and are heavy laden, and I will give you rest" (Matthew 11:28). Since the early dawn of mankind's history, when our Eden of bliss became a desert of discord, we have been creatures of restlessness. When we are bereft of the peace that comes from God through the saving grace of Christ, we become fish out of water.

Divorce, alcoholism and immorality are direct results of the restlessness of sin. This diabolical unrest has permeated our nation like a contagious disease and has become the underlying cause of domestic, community and social problems. The basic cause of our national immorality is this spiritual unrest in people's lives today.

In my travels about the country I have sensed unrest in almost every phase of our modern-day living. This changeable, unsettled, roving, transient, sleepless and fidgety spirit is due primarily to the restlessness of the human heart and its separation from the Christ of tranquility and peace. These insecure individuals could find spiritual peace and physical rest by surrendering their lives to Jesus Christ.

The Bible says, "The wicked are like the troubled sea." Every day I come in contact with mixed-up, paradoxical men and women: rich people who are held in the grip of insecurity; intellectual people who have lost their way; strong people who live in fear of weakness and defeat. I long to take every one of them by the hand and lead them into the presence of the Savior who said, "Come unto me, all ye that labor and are heavy laden, and I will give you rest."

Hear and accept the divine invitation today: "Come unto me, and rest!"

But rest is not all that weary people need. Other invitations to happiness await the distressed who will dare to follow Christ.

A second invitation is to discipleship.

"Jesus said to them, 'Follow Me, and I will make you become fishers of men'" (Mark 1:17). We are saved to serve; we are redeemed to reproduce spiritually; we are fished out of the miry clay so that we in turn may become fishers of men.

This invitation to discipleship is the most thrilling ever to come to mankind. Just imagine being a working partner with God in the redemption of the world! Jesus challenged, "If anyone serves Me, let him follow Me; and where I am, there My servant will be also. If anyone serves Me, him My Father will honor" (John 12:26).

Christian discipleship gives us the privilege of being associated with Christ intimately. And the faithful discharging of the glorious responsibilities of true discipleship invokes the approval and favor of God Himself.

Would you like to "lay up for yourselves treasures in heaven"? (Matthew 6:20). Then, Christian, take off your coat of pious indifference, roll up your sleeves of Christian fervor and go to work in the teeming vineyard of souls. Opportunities lie all around you. Your neighbors are without Christ, your children are unsaved, your colleagues are waiting to see Jesus in you. I challenge you in Christ's name to become an effective, efficient, fishers of men.

"I am interested," you say, "but how may I be a disciple of Christ?" The answer must come from God's Word itself. "If anyone desires to come after me," said Jesus, "let him deny himself, and take up his cross daily, and follow Me" (Luke 9:23). Before you can follow Jesus in discipleship, the selfish, sinful "self" must be crucified, so that Christ is pre-eminent in your heart and life.

Jesus also said, "If you abide in My word, then you are My disciples indeed" (John 8:31). Disciple literally means "a learner, a student, a follower." Salvation may be instantaneous, but discipleship must be learned from the master teacher, Christ Himself. We must know the Word before we can teach the Word. So, the second requirement of discipleship is that we continue in the Word of God.

Also from the lips of Jesus we hear, "By this My Father is glorified, that you bear much fruit; so you will be My disciples" (John 15:8). If self is slain and the Spirit reigns, the fruits of discipleship are bound to be seen in our lives. A true disciple of Christ will bear the fruit of the Spirit, which is "love, joy, peace, longsuffering, gentleness, goodness, faith, meekness, and temperance" (Galatians 5:22-23). People who contact us daily will take note that we have been with Jesus. We will radiate Christ. The secret of the Christian life is Christ in us, producing fruit.

The third invitation is to live in the realm of God.

Jesus said, "Abide in Me, and I in you" (John 15:4). Personal salvation is not an occasional rendezvous with Deity; it is an actual dwelling with God. Christianity is not just an avocation; it is a lifelong, eternity-long vocation. David, thrilled with the knowledge that his life was in God, said in Psalm 91:1—"He who dwells in the secret place of the Most High shall abide under the shadow of the Almighty."

If you read and reread this beautiful psalm, you will discover that in Him we have a permanent abode and residence, and that all of the comfort, security and affection that the human heart craves is found in Him.

Modern psychiatrists say that one of the basic needs of mankind is security. In this Psalm, we are assured that in God we have the greatest of security: "No evil shall befall you, nor shall any plague come near your dwelling; for He shall give His angels charge over you, to keep you in all your ways" (Psalm 91:10-11).

Another basic need is affection. Those who "abide in Him" are the objects of God's affection and love. The Bible says, "Because he has set his love upon Me, therefore I will deliver him; I will set him on high, because he has known My name" (Psalm 91:14).

No greater demonstration of love has ever been witnessed by the world than God's love manifested in His Son, Jesus Christ. The very center of the whole Gospel message is summed up in those divinely significant words: "But God demonstrates His own love toward us, in that while we were still sinners, Christ died for us" (Romans 5:8).

You cannot say that you are friendless when Christ has said, "No longer do I call you servants … but I have called you friends" (John 15:15). If you lament the fact that you have been bereft of affection and love in this life, I happily commend Christ. He loved you enough to lay down His life for you. Not only that, but by His atonement upon the cross He purchased the favor of God on your behalf, and now through Him you may be the recipient of the grace and love of God without measure.

Another basic need that will be fulfilled by our dwelling and abiding in God is the need to belong. In all three invitations that we have discussed, we find God through Christ inviting sinful men and women to be identified with Him in His great redemptive and creative work. No club of any kind in this world can compare with the knowledge of the fact that you belong to God and are identified with Him.

These three invitations are not mine. They are given by Jesus Himself. No man or woman has ever found complete rest apart from Christ. To the multitudes of distressed, troubled and weary He beckons, "Come unto me … and I will give you rest."[2]

Rejoice, dear reader turned reformer. You are about to embark on the most thrilling and rewarding venture of your entire life.

In the next chapter, you will be invited to embrace God's love and learn more of what it means for you personally.

PART THREE

EXPERIENCING LOVE

"Hope does not put us to shame, because God's love has been poured into our hearts through the Holy Spirit who has been given to us."

Romans 5:5

CHAPTER NINE

Reveling in God's Love

God has designed everything in the natural world to reveal the mysteries of the spiritual world. Proverbs 25:2 states "It is the glory of God to conceal things, but the glory of kings is to search things out."

Kings, Priests, Sons, and Daughters

The Bible implicitly refers to those who have placed their faith in Christ as kings and priests. 1 Peter 2:9 proclaims "But you are a chosen race, a royal priesthood, a holy nation, a people for his own possession, that you may proclaim the excellencies of him who called you out of darkness into his marvelous light." While we live out our life on earth, we are kings and priests in training—we are being prepared for our future role as joint heirs with Jesus, the King of kings.

The Bible also refers to believers as *sons* and *children of God*. Jesus, the Son of God, is considered the first born among many brothers according to Romans 8:29. We who place our faith in Christ are considered His brothers. Romans 8:14-18 explains:

> For all who are led by the Spirit of God are sons of God
> … but you have received the Spirit of adoption as sons, by
> whom we cry, "Abba! Father!" The Spirit himself bears
> witness with our spirit that we are children of God, and if
> children, then heirs—heirs of God and fellow heirs with
> Christ, provided we suffer with him in order that we may
> also be glorified with him. For I consider that the
> sufferings of this present time are not worth comparing
> with the glory that is to be revealed to us. For the creation
> waits with eager longing for the revealing of the sons of
> God.[1]

To be loved by God the Father as a son or daughter is to experience unconditional love, protection, and provision. As God's children, we are His responsibility. Our role is to grow up as children of God, following in the example of our Brother, Jesus, as we live on earth. The way of Jesus is love. We are to love the Lord our God with all our heart, soul, mind, and strength. Additionally, we are to love our neighbors as ourselves (Deuteronomy 6:5, Mark 12:30-31, Luke 10:27, and Matthew 22:37). To follow Jesus' example means to also love our enemies (Matthew 5:43-48 and Luke 6:27-36).

Our life on earth is our time of preparation for our eternal future when we will meet God our Father face to face.

The Church—Christ's Bride

Elsewhere in Scriptures, all believers who comprise the Church are collectively referred to as the *Bride of Christ*. We learn from Ephesians 5:25-

27 Jesus, *the Bridegroom*, has sacrificially and lovingly chosen the Church to be His bride.

In all these descriptions of Believers—kings, priests, sons, bride—God reveals a desire for deep, abiding relationship. Christianity is considered a religion. However, it is not a religion of requirements, but rather one of relationship—relationship that influences our behavior.

Sacrificial Love

Certainly, in the natural world, marriage is the most intimate relationship humans can enjoy. With our spouses, we enjoy communication and emotional connection on a much deeper level than with our friends or acquaintances. For God to refer to the Church as the Bride of Christ reveals God wants an intimate spiritual relationship with us. Furthermore, as the Husband, Jesus is the example of how to live our new life in love.

The apostle Paul instructed believers to be imitators of God, as beloved children—beloved children in contrast to workers seeking to earn a wage. The love God has for us is completely and continually poured out for us. God's love is not something our conduct alters. The apostle Paul instructs believers to walk in love as Christ loved us and gave Himself up as our substitute sacrifice (Ephesians 5:1-2). Self-sacrificial love is the necessary component for a holy lifestyle ideally demonstrated in marriage as ordained by God.

Ephesians 5:22-33 provides instruction for wives and husbands to best enjoy holy matrimony as God intended. From this passage, we learn that God intends mutual submission between wives and husbands with specific instruction to the husband to love his wife as Christ loved the Church. Christ's love for the Church was supremely expressed as He willingly suffered and died for her (the Church), that He might sanctify her, so that He can present the Church to Himself.

The Wedding Supper of the Lamb

Jesus is also known as the *Lamb of God*, referring to His sacrifice paying the debt of sin to restore all who believe in Him to God. In the last book of the Bible, Revelation, we learn of the *wedding supper of the Lamb* when the Bride of Christ and Jesus are forever united (Revelation 19:6-9). Perfect union with Jesus personally and participation in His holiness, joy, glory, and kingdom reign are included in the symbol of marriage.

There is no human relationship more intimate than that of husband and wife. There is no love more passionate than the love of husband and wife. References to marriage are used many times in the New Testament as a depiction of the believer's relationship with Christ. Marriage as an analogy is especially meaningful in light of the traditional Jewish wedding customs. The people of Jesus' day would have readily understood the parallels. However, we must search to learn the depth of meaning Jesus intentionally communicated.

Traditional Jewish Matrimonial Customs

In ancient Jewish tradition, the father of the groom commonly selected a bride for his son. The father sent a servant to a nearby village to discover a suitable bride, usually a woman the son had never met. The servant would then offer the potential bride's family a proposal. If the bride's father deemed the proposal suitable, the bride then had the opportunity to accept or reject the offer. Upon acceptance, the servant gave the *groom's gift* as a payment to the bride's family but ultimately, the sum belonged to the bride.

The groom's gift changed the bride's status and set her free from her parent's household. The servant then went back with the news to the father. Once the groom's father approved the choice of the bride, the bridegroom would go to meet his bride-to-be for the first time. At that point, the groom paid a *Mohar* or *bride-price* (like the ring for modern marriage ceremonies) and declared in a loud voice, "The price has been paid in full" in front of the village. At this point, the *Ketubah* document (or covenant promise) was drawn up specifying the groom would provide for all the needs of the bride during the betrothal period.

Once signed, the bridegroom declared in a loud voice, "It is finished." The groom would then give a speech of promise. He would say, "I have to go. I'm going to prepare the *Chuppah* (bridal chamber), a place for you at my father's house." The bride would respond "Do not go." The groom would reply, "It is better for you that I'll go but I will come back." "When?" she'd ask. And the groom would respond, "I do not know, nor the servant, only my father knows the day."

This began the betrothal period, which was binding on both the bride and groom. The betrothal was so binding the couple would need a religious divorce or to get an order to annul the contract. The option for divorce or annulment was only available to the husband—the wife had no say.

During the betrothal period the bride and groom were separated until the wedding day. Jewish customs reveal the responsibility of the bride during the betrothal period is to be faithful to the groom (2 Corinthians 11:2 and Ephesians 5:24) while she prepares herself and awaits the groom's return. The primary purpose of the separation was two-fold: to give the bride time to prepare herself to leave all that she'd known and to fully identify with her betrothed husband, and to allow the groom time build the addition to his father's house where the two would live after the wedding.

Constructing a suitable dwelling could require one to two years. Determination of when the dwelling place was ready to receive the bride was the responsibility of the father, not the groom. During the time of preparation, the bride and her bridesmaids constructed her holy garments for the upcoming wedding. During the groom's absence, the groom assigned one of his servants to the bride to insure she was cared for and watchful for the return of the groom. Because the bridegroom would usually show up at midnight, the bride had to have her oil lamp burning all the time. The bride also had other virgins helping and serving her anticipating the wedding.

Upon the night of the groom's return one of the groom's party went ahead of the bridegroom, leading the way to the bride's house shouting, "Behold, the bridegroom comes." This would be followed by the sounding of the shofar. At the sounding of the shofar, the entire wedding processional would go through the streets of the city to the bride's house.

Marriage as Ordained by God

God's institution of holy matrimony on earth was to be a one-time, life-long commitment between one man and one woman who came together in marriage as virgins. The only grounds God permits for divorce is sexual infidelity. Even so, God is clear about divorce stating that He hates divorce (Malachi 2:16). Divorce is devastating to all involved, especially children. Any deviation from His design is abhorrent to Him. Marriage is not a contract; it is a covenant. Divorce destroys the whole concept of covenant—covenant is exceedingly important to God. God wants every Christian marriage to be a picture of the relationship of Jesus Christ to His Bride, the Church.

Marriage is the highest and holiest relationship God instituted for humanity. Marriage is also the earthly depiction of the kind of committed, eternal, spiritual relationship we are to have with God. Is it any wonder why the enemy of God has worked so hard to destroy marriage as God intended?

In our western culture all attention is given to the bride. However, in ancient Jewish tradition, emphasis was on the groom. Once the bride accepted the groom's marriage proposal, she had no option of cancelling or annulling it—only the groom has this option. This illustrates the spiritual covenant God has made with us. We are the Bride, we are not to seek divorce from God. If we lose our way and become unfaithful to God, He will forever remain faithful to us and seek to draw us back. Jesus is the Groom who will not break His word.

Discovering the Meaning of the Mystery

Let's consider the richness of the mysteries revealed in the traditional Jewish marriage.

- *The father of the groom selected the bride for the Son.* We were chosen from before the foundation of the world (see Ephesians 1:4).
- *The father sent a servant ahead for the groom to find his bride.* God sent John the Baptist to prepare the people to receive the Lamb of God (John 1:29).
- *The father presents the proposal to the intended bride.* The gospel of Jesus is the proposal for our redemption (Mark 1:15).
- *Upon acceptance, the bride is given a gift.* Salvation is our gift the moment we receive Jesus as our Personal Savior (2 Corinthians 5:17).

- *Upon receipt of the groom's gift, the bride's status sets her free from her family of origin.* The moment we place our faith in Jesus, we transferred from the citizenry of the world to the citizenry of heaven (Ephesians 2:19).

- *The servant went back with news to the Father.* Jesus was resurrected and has ascended to the right hand of the Father (Acts 2:33).

- *The covenant promise is established indicating that the Bridegroom will attend to the provisions of the Bride until his return.* Jesus promised He would not leave us as orphans, but He would send the Holy Spirit to help us in every way (John 14:8-21).

- *The groom paid a bride-price and declared in a loud voice, "The price has been paid in full" followed by the words "It is finished."* Jesus personally paid the debt of sin in full and declared "It is finished" before dying on the cross (John 19:30).

- *The groom announces he must leave while the bride asks him to stay. Yet, he declares it is better for the bride that he leaves.* Jesus declared it was for our advantage that He leave and in His absence He said He would send the Holy Spirit to watch over us (John 16:7).

- *The groom leaves to go to his father's house to prepare a house for his bride.* Jesus left to His Father's house to prepare our rooms (John 14:2).

- *The bride asks when he will return. The groom replies he does not know, nor does his servant, only his father.* When Jesus' disciples asked about His return, Jesus stated, "But concerning that day and hour no one knows, not even the angels of heaven, nor the Son, but the Father only" (Matthew 24:36).

- *During the time of separation, the bride is to be preparing herself to meet her groom.* In the parable of the Ten Virgins, we learn the importance of being ready at all times (Matthew 25:1-13).

Truly, we must spend our time wisely preparing ourselves for Christ's return. Scriptures indicate He will not return for a Bride with spots and wrinkles. We are to be cooperating with the sanctifying work of the Holy Spirit so we can best be prepared to reign and rule as kings and priests, to enjoy God's love as sons and daughters and to be the Bride of Christ adorned in fine white linen.

> Then I heard what seemed to be the voice of a great
> multitude, like the roar of many waters and like the sound
> of mighty peals of thunder, crying out,
> "Hallelujah!
> For the Lord our God
>   the Almighty reigns.
> Let us rejoice and exult
>   and give him the glory,
> for the marriage of the Lamb has come,
>   and his Bride has made herself ready;
> it was granted her to clothe herself
>   with fine linen, bright and pure"—
> for the fine linen is the righteous deeds of the saints"
> And the angel said to me, "Write this: Blessed are
> those who are invited to the marriage supper of the
> Lamb." And he said to me, "These are the true words of
> God."[2]

If we are cooperative in the process, we will enjoy the maximum benefits of a believer beginning here in this life. Searching out the things of God is truly to our benefit.

In the next chapter, you will learn how to effectively persevere in your faith until you reach the victory Christ promises.

CHAPTER TEN

Persevere in God's Love

I trust by now you're enjoying a new-found sense of purpose. I sincerely hope so. Yet, it's important for me to make certain you are more fully prepared to successfully step out in your calling.

As a new creature in Christ, you have a new eternal spirit, you have the indwelling of the Holy Spirit, and you have your assignment from God to help His will to be done. This makes you, along with all believers, a target for the enemy of God. You will experience opposition. However, you are fully equipped to do God's will and have victory over the enemy.

Now, armed with truth, you can be part of the reformation the world needs. As believers united together, we are not only ambassadors for Christ, we are all part of His army. However, Christ's army functions entirely differently than the world's militia. Our mode of operation is based in love. God's people are to be known by their love, which is His love flowing through us.

Edwin Markham wrote the famous poem, "Outwitted," which exemplifies the way God's army must operate:

He drew a circle that shut me out-

Heretic, rebel, a thing to flout.

But love and I had the wit to win:

We drew a circle and took him in!

As believers, our new purpose in life is to draw others to the same saving knowledge of Jesus and God's love we've been blessed to find. In truth, we've become a part of God's army in fighting the spiritual battle over human souls.

Scripture explains all creation is temporal, whereas all that is spiritual is eternal. The spirit world then is more "real" than our physical world. From the beginning, Satan set out to destroy all that is good in God's sight. Satan honed right in on the most valuable target, the human spirit—created by God for communion with Him. Satan succeeded, which means every human being born since the first man and woman is part of a very real spiritual battle.

As believers, we will encounter the enemy's wrath in a variety of ways, but Jesus has already overcome the enemy. We do not operate *for* victory—we operate *from* victory. This reality must be firmly implanted in the depths of our understanding. We must confidently know who we are in Christ. We must live out our new lives in Christ as God instructs, so we will not only enjoy the victorious life Christ died to provide us, but we will exemplify Jesus by the way we interact with others.

The way Jesus lived and interacted with people is our example. Believers who confidently know their position and authority in Christ, who rely on the indwelling Holy Spirit by listening and following His instructions, are those who manifest God's love and plans in such ways others are positively impacted. The Holy Spirit is the same power who raised Christ from the dead. The apostle John wrote, "Little children, you are from God and have overcome them, [those of the world] for he who is in you [the Holy Spirit] is greater than he who is in the world [Satan]" (1 John 4:4) [added words mine].

Believers in Christ have their citizenship transferred from the world to heaven the moment they place their faith in Christ. We are no longer of the world gravely influenced by Satan. While we live out the remainder of our physical existence, we are to be Christ's change agents, sharing God's truth and love with all who are yet to be reborn. We reform the lost and dying world from the influence of evil to that of God's love—one person at a time.

We remain in the world, but we no longer belong to the world. God has given us everything we need to successfully live according to the new creatures we are. Of course, since we remain on the earth influenced by sin, we too will be adversely impacted by sin—sin we commit or sin committed by others. But, we have everything we need to overcome sin, always at our disposal. The Bible speaks of the life of Christians on earth as being a war—a war against good and evil, a war between God and Satan. Understand Christ has already fully defeated Satan.

God's Ways are Higher than Man's Ways

Many people question why a good God would allow suffering and evil to continue in the world. People also question the claim Jesus has fully defeated the enemy, in light of the continuing evil in the world. These are both legitimate questions, the answers for which are found in the Bible. In fact, Christian theism is the only worldview that can consistently make sense of the problem of evil and suffering.

Everything God does is motivated by His love. In everything God does, He has a good plan and purpose. Nothing happens on earth or in heaven outside God's sovereign authority. If God chooses to permit something, even something evil, He does so for an infinitely wise reason. We need to know God is sovereign over Satan. The very suffering of Jesus—all that He endured leading up to and including death by crucifixion—brought victory over Satan.

Some may ask, "If God has the power and authority over Satan, why didn't He simply wipe Satan out?" God has the right and power to do this, and Revelation 20:10 reveals there is a day appointed for this to happen. What we need to understand is that God has a good and perfect plan and purpose in allowing Satan to ravage humanity for centuries.

Colossians 1:16 states, "For by him [Jesus], all things were created, in heaven and on earth, visible and invisible, whether thrones or dominions or rulers or authorities—all things were created through him and for him" [added words mine]. *All things* created includes every human being ever planned by God to be born. As we suffer in life, and respond to the suffering the same way Jesus did—trusting God for the good to come— then we magnify the glory of Christ. Romans 8:16-17 assures us, "The Spirit himself bears witness with our spirit that we are children of God, and if children, then heirs—heirs of God and fellow-heirs with Christ, provided we suffer with him in order that we may also be glorified with him."

Jesus made clear as recorded in John 16:33, "In the world you will have tribulation [pain and suffering]. But take heart; I have overcome the world" [added words mine]. Just as Jesus' suffering produced good, so does our suffering. We have God's promise in Romans 8:28, "And we know that for those who love God, all things work together for good, for those who are called according to his purpose."

John Piper is the founder and teacher of DesiringGod.org and chancellor of Bethlehem College and Seminary. For thirty-three years, he served as pastor of Bethlehem Baptist Church, Minneapolis, Minnesota. He is the author of more than fifty books, and of countless articles. References to his work in this book are used with permission. In Piper's teaching entitled, "The Fall of Satan and the Victory of Christ," he explains:

> Satan and all his pain, serves in the end to magnify the power and wisdom and love and grace and mercy and patience and wrath of Jesus Christ. We would not know Jesus in the fullness of His glory if he had not defeated Satan the way He did. Jesus will be more highly honored in the end because He defeats Satan through longsuffering, patience, humility, servanthood, suffering, and death, rather through raw power. The more highly honored the Son is, the greater the joy for those who love Him.

How to Relate to Evil:

1. *Expect* evil. "Do not be surprised at the fiery trial when it comes upon you to test you, as though something strange were happening to you" (1 Peter 4:12).

2. *Endure* evil. "Love bears all thing, believes all things, hopes all things, endures all things" (1 Corinthians 13:7; cf. Mark 13:13).

3. *Give thanks* for the refining effect of evil that comes against you. "Give thanks always and for everything to God the Father in the name of our Lord Jesus Christ" (Ephesians 5:20; cf. 1 Thessalonians 5:18; Romans 5:3-5).

4. *Hate* evil. "Let love be genuine. *Abhor* what is evil; hold fast to what is good" (Romans 12:9).

5. *Pray for escape* from evil. "Lead us not into temptation, but deliver us from evil" (Matthew 6:13).

6. *Expose* evil. "Take no part in the unfruitful works of darkness, but instead expose them" (Ephesians 5:11).

7. *Overcome* evil with good. "Do not be overcome by evil, but overcome evil with good" (Romans 12:21).

8. *Resist* evil. "Resist the devil and he will flee from you" (James 4:7).

But, on the other hand:

1. Never despair that this evil world is out of God's control. "[He] works all things according to the counsel of his will" (Ephesians 1:11).

2. Never give in to the sense that because of random evil life is absurd and meaningless. "How unsearchable are his judgments and how inscrutable his ways! . . . For from him and through him and to him are all things. To him be glory forever" (Romans 11:33,36).

3. Never yield to the thought that God sins, or is ever unjust or unrighteous in the way he governs the universe. "The Lord is righteous in all his ways." (Psalm 145:17).

4. Never doubt that God is totally for you in Christ. If you trust him with your life, you are in Christ. Never doubt that all the evil that befalls you—even if it takes your life—is God's loving, purifying, saving, fatherly discipline. It is not an expression of his punishment in wrath. That fell on Jesus Christ our substitute. "The Lord disciplines the one he loves, and chastises every son whom he receives" (Hebrews 12:6).[1]

Satan intends his evil to defeat us. However, once we have a proper understanding of the reality of God *in our suffering,* we have an understanding how to endure. By our response, Jesus' glory is magnified, and faith is accounted to us, which pleases God. Hebrews 11:6 states, "And without faith it is impossible to please him, for whoever would draw near to God must believe that he exists and that he rewards those who seek him."

Jesus' Compassion Reveals God's Love

While the suffering of believers will be used for good, suffering is not God's perfect will for humanity. God created Adam and Eve in the Garden of Eden where there was no suffering. The rejection of God by the first man and woman brought suffering into the world. In response to the rejection, God promised a Redeemer—ultimately Jesus, the Second Person of the Trinity. During Jesus' human existence, there were countless times He was moved with compassion. The love of God for His people was then made evident through miracles, signs, and wonders. Jesus performed miracles of various sorts that alleviated pain and suffering.

The miracles Jesus performed, motivated by God's love, were also performed by His disciples once they learned how to hear and obey God and then step out in faith. In John 14:12-14, Jesus says, "Truly, truly, I say to you, whoever believes in me will also do the works that I do; and greater works than these will he do, because I am going to the Father. Whatever you ask in my name, this I will do, that the Father may be glorified in the Son. If you ask me anything in my name, I will do it." Believers today have the same ability through the power of the Holy Spirit.

My firm belief is when we suffer, we need to ask God for any understanding He may impart. God may reveal the source of the suffering as a bad choice we made or a matter we need to repent of. He may reveal the source by way of another person. By revealing the source, He is often providing us a way of escape. The miracles Jesus and His disciples performed as recorded in the Bible, and the many verified miracles Jesus' followers have performed ever since, include miracles for healing, for provision, for relationships, and even for restoring people from physical death. How to find solutions for suffering is the main focus in the second book in this series, *Renew Your Hope! Remedy for Personal Breakthroughs*. Because God loves us, He wants the best for us. He loves when we seek Him and, Hebrews 11:6 reveals that when we seek Him, He rewards us. The "reward" may not be exactly what we wanted. However, the reward will be good and perfect, coming from God.

The greatest expression of God's love was in the life, death, and resurrection of Jesus. The apostle John wrote in John 15:13: "Greater love has no one than this, that someone lay down his life for his friends." Jesus, the Son of God, willingly endured tremendous suffering, even death by crucifixion, motivated by God's eternal love for us, so that we could be set free from the devastation of the enemy whose entire focus is to steal, kill and destroy. The key to our victory is to be united in Christ.

United in God's Love

Deception (or lying) is the primary strategy of the devil to keep people from being united with God, through faith in Christ. In fact, the Bible refers to Satan as the father of all lies. I firmly believe more people today are deceived than any other time in my life. The most powerful weapon in spiritual warfare is truth. As recorded in John 8:31-32, Jesus said, "If you abide in my word, you are truly my disciples, and you will know the truth and the truth will set you free." The truth includes the reality that unity is power; division is impotence. No wonder the enemy works overtime to divide believers who have the power of truth.

Deception and division certainly characterize the state of our world today. The devil has made great inroads dividing people in a variety of ways. But armed with the knowledge of the devil's tactics, we believers must diligently work to promote unity. The best way for believers all over the world to become united is by prayer. Prayer is our supreme weapon of spiritual warfare. (Practical aspects of prayer are discussed in chapter eleven.)

The enemy knows the power of the Holy Spirit. He knows if believers truly understood the impact available to them by uniting in purpose and Spirit, his work would be destroyed. When believers, confident of who they are in Christ, unite and pray in the fullness of their authority, God orders His angels to war with the enemy. Our war is not against flesh and blood. Certainly, the enemy influences people to do evil, destructive things. However, Satan and his minions are the instigators of the evil. Our battle is a spiritual battle. Satan is at war for our minds, to lie to us, and to convince us of all things contrary to the Word of God. We engage in counter-attacks by keeping our mind fixed on Christ and the truth of God's Word. We battle by deliberately replacing all deceptive thoughts and conclusions with truth, and by purposefully dwelling in Christ. We must be intentional about remaining in truth, so our faith is based on a solid foundation.

One prayer I'd like all Christians to pray is to ask God to reveal all corruption and lies creating division. Ask God to bring evil to light so believers can combat deception with righteousness. Pray asking God to reveal where we have corrupt leaders or people of influence and pray to remove them from office and to replace them with godly men and women who are obedient to God's will.

God's Word instructs us to love one another and to love our human enemies. Only God knows which of our enemies will come to the light of truth, repent, believe in, and receive Christ. So, we must pray for all unbelievers, even those who are against us. Before we placed our faith in Christ, we too were enemies of God, and His love drew us in. Love and prayer are the strategies for Christians to bring about the godly reformation our world needs.

Uniting in God's Purpose

By now, I hope you realize God intends you to be part of a great movement—one that brings hope for our future and that assures true personal fulfillment. You should experience an excitement in knowing you are called by God for a specific purpose in your life. You are unique, so the contribution you can make on earth for God's kingdom is unique. Understand all believers are collectively referred to as the *Body of Christ*. And just as the human body has many members, each with different functions, so we need each part of the Body of Christ to do its part in order for the entire body to properly function. The apostle Paul wrote about how we are to experience unity with diversity as one body in 1 Corinthians 12:18 "God arranged the members in the body, each one of them, as he chose." Your created purpose was established by God, and when you live accordingly, you please Him.

Your God-given purpose is often referred to as your *call* or *calling*. Discovering your created purpose is not difficult, yet actually doing so is something too few people accomplish. To help you, I've provided some guidelines for discovering your created purpose and how to best function in your calling. You need to consider both your natural talents and the spiritual gifts God has given you to identify your call. Your call will always match your deepest desire because God places His desires in our hearts. Whatever you are deeply passionate about is evidence of the direction for your life and the purpose you are to fulfill in God's plan.

The process of discovering your call will likely include inquiring of others to learn what they see in you as your natural talents, looking within to identify your genuine passion and, praying to God to reveal your spiritual gifts. With these three firmly identified, you need to get prepared to fulfill your call.

I have the gift of administration. Organizing and identifying how to get from point A to point Z and maintaining awareness how each step impacts the whole is a gift I enjoy. If you are not wired that way, what follows in the next few sections will be helpful. Believers could take a lesson from successful businesses by having a plan. While there are many schools of thought about what is needed in a business plan, what I offer is geared to you fulfilling your God-given purpose. You may wish to obtain the help of your pastor or another mature believer who knows you and can help you in the process of clearly identifying your call as well as the methods you'll implement to fulfill your call.

Own Your God-Given Vision

You don't want to have a vague sense of your calling. You want to be as complete in your understanding of God's purpose for you as possible. However, like Abraham, God may not tell you what the end result is to be, only to reveal details during the journey. God told Abraham to leave his family and go to the land He would show him. Abraham (then named Abram) set out in obedience not knowing where he was going. Faith is going to be essential as you step into your calling.

However, having as much of a plan as possible is wise. As is often said, "Failing to plan is planning to fail." And since we're exploring your particular calling in God's plan, I know you don't want to fail. Not that you won't make mistakes along the way. We all do. However, simply by making a plan, we can minimize mistakes. Mistakes are not an indication of failure. Doing nothing is the definition of failure where kingdom work is concerned.

I suggest you start by prayerfully creating a vision statement. Being as thorough as possible, write out what you understand your call to be. As you pray for the Lord's help, you'll eventually come up with a good statement. Don't think what you write is set in stone. The Lord may reveal more details to you in the journey that makes amending your vision statement prudent.

Following is my current vision statement:

> Pamela Christian Ministries' vision is to be an asset to the Church, redeeming its relevancy through media to reach the postmodern, relativistic mindset of people who are lost to the truth of Jesus.

My original vision statement was limited to the geography of the United States. But in recent years, the Lord has revealed my reach will be extended, so I amended my vision statement. A vision statement should communicate your vision (passion), what you intend to accomplish, an overview of how you intend to accomplish your vision and the people or groups you intend to reach.

Once you are convinced you know and can properly articulate your vision, you're in a position to network with others to find a place where you can get to work. Your efforts won't feel like work because you will be doing what you're passionate about. You may have a place to fulfill your vision within your own home church or another existing organization. Or, you may be like me and sense the Lord calling you to start a new ministry. In any event, share your vision with your pastor so you can get the guidance and prayer covering you'll need.

Know Your Mission

Being confident about your vision will help you better embrace your mission. If you are seeking to join an existing church or organization where you can lend your talents and gifts, you'd be wise to learn about their mission statement before committing to serve.

A mission statement reveals the company's/church's/organization's goals, ethics, culture, and norms for decision-making. Mission statements, if created correctly, will fully support the vision of the organization's goals. The mission statement provides parameters that will help identify the specific actions/activities the company/church/organization will engage in.

If you are being called by God to start a ministry, then you will want to develop and write down your own mission statement. A mission statement can be as little as one sentence, but shouldn't be more than three or four sentences. The apostle Paul summarized his mission by claiming "I became a minister [of the church] … to make the word of God fully known … that we may present everyone mature in Christ" (Colossians 1:25-28) [added words mine].

LifeWay, a company that provides Christian Bibles, books, and other recourses in retail stores, published a good list of the benefits of having a written mission statement:

- Your personal mission puts limits on your ministry.

- When you lead within the limits of your personal mission, your motives and attitude will usually be good. You will serve more easily and effectively.

- Your personal mission also gives you a sense of security.

- You know you are pleasing God so you can relax. You are not trying to please people and are not stressed by demands you cannot meet. You have a sense of purpose and intentionality. You know you are working from your strengths.

- Focusing on your personal mission helps alleviate jealousy and competition in ministry.

- You know your mission and by implication know others have different missions. You are not competing with anyone. Your only competition is with your own God-produced personal standards, expectations, and potentialities.[2]

- Mission statements are biblical.

- Mission statements help you identify your essential ministry.

- Mission statements make it possible for you to make an effective difference.

Interim Ministry Partners, a Division of HOPE Network, list their "top seven" reasons why every ministry should have an explicit, clear, specific mission statement, adapted from their article "Why Bother With A Mission Statement?" (http://interimministrypartners.com/why-bother-with-a-mission-statement/).

My personal mission statement is "God has called and equipped me to teach others from His Word through speaking and writing via various media, so that others can discover and live in life-giving truth—specifically through faith in and knowledge of Jesus."

Assess Your Season of Life

Your season of life will directly impact the specific actions you take in fulfilling your call. Let's say you've learned your natural talents consist of singing and teaching and your spiritual gifts include administration and faith. Let's also say God has revealed to you your calling is to reach great numbers of people for Him through serving at your home church. If your season in life means you have a great deal of free time, and assuming you have expertise in singing, you might approach your pastor and offer to establish a new choir. Your natural talent, education, and gifts of administration and faith to establish something new would all be utilized.

On the other hand, if you are young, newly married, or have small children, your season might be better spent getting additional musical training, writing music, singing in the choir, and otherwise preparing for a day where you can do more. Always pray, asking God what His desire is for you to fulfill your call given the current season of your life.

Many people get excited about their call and seek to reach the end goal, without assessing their season of life. Haste will always produce frustration and the need to go back to step one to walk out the calling in its proper succession. God is gracious. If we miss the mark, He doesn't revoke the call on our life. He simply takes us back to the place on the path where we veered off and gives us as many chances to get success as we need. However, take care not to be like the Israelites who wandered in the desert forty years on their way to the Promised Land—a trek that should have only taken days. The Israelites complaining and murmuring prevented them from the success God had in mind for them.

Set Goals

Establishing goals to achieve your objective is always wise. In fact, studies have been demonstrated those who write down their goals are among the most successful.

Forbes online magazine reports a study about goal-setting conducted in the Harvard MBA Program. Harvard's graduate students were essentially asked the following questions:

- Do you have a set of goals for your future?
- Are your goals placed in writing?
- What plans or strategies do you have to translate your goals into reality?

The results of the study revealed only three percent of the students had their goals in writing, as well as having specific plans to accomplish their goals. Thirteen percent had goals in mind, but had not written them down. Whereas, eighty-four percent of the students surveyed had no goals at all.

After ten years the same students were interviewed again. The conclusion of the study was astonishing. Those from the thirteen percent group, who had unwritten goals, earned twice the amount of wages as those from the eighty-four percent group who had no particular goals. However, those from the three percent group, with written goals and specific plans to achieve their goals, were earning, on average, ten times as much as the other two groups, combined.[3]

Ask yourself which of the three groups in the study are you in? If you've not been inclined to write down your goals, I strongly suggest you take up the habit. You may have a particular destination or end result in mind and a general idea of how to reach the destination. However, your level of confidence will be increased, and your potential for making wrong turns will be minimized if you have goal-markers to reach your intended destination.

Naturally, if you are serving at your church or with an existing organization, goal setting will need to be done in the context of their mission statement and consistent with your role in serving.

When establishing your goals, I suggest the following:

- **Be in prayer.** Ask the Lord to reveal the best goals for you to have to accomplish His will for your life. Ask questions such as:
    - o Will I be serving only in my country or will I be serving in other countries?
    - o Do I need to get a passport, learn another language, get a higher level of education in any area?
    - o What resources do I need to accomplish the end goal?
    - o What are the best incremental steps to take to help reach the end goal?
- **Write down your specific goals.** You are setting goals so you don't operate from a vague sense of reaching your objective, and to increase your level of success. The more specific each goal is, the more direction you have.
- **Put deadlines on your written goals.** Without deadlines, you can suffer otherwise unnecessary delays and frustration. Make sure your deadlines are realistic. Unrealistic deadlines can also produce unnecessary delays and frustration.
- **Include a strategy for reaching your goals.** Under each goal write at least three specific steps you will take to accomplish the goal.

At this point, you've discovered your God-given purpose, you've determined your talents and gifts, you have articulated your vision, and you have some idea what you will be doing and how. What you can expect as you step into your calling is the subject of the next chapter.

CHAPTER ELEVEN

Being Transformed by God's Love

Experiencing God's love is our aim. Many people, even those who profess to be Christian, do not experience God's love. They have knowledge about God's love, but they do not experience that love as they can.

John Piper, in his article "How is God's Love Experienced in the Heart?" writes:

> Experiencing the love of God, not just thinking about it, is something we should desire with all our hearts. This is an experience of great joy because in it we taste the very reality of God and His love. It is the ground of deep and wonderful assurance—the assurance that our hope "will not disappoint us" (Romans 5:5). This assurance helps us "exult in the hope of the glory of God" (Romans 5:2). It carries us through terrible trials of faith.[1]

What? Terrible trials of faith? Yes, your faith will be tested. Does that make God a bully? No, we've already established God is love. Many things are strengthened and improved by opposition. The same is true of our faith—our faith in who God is, faith in who we are in Christ, and faith that God will do what He says He will do. Chapter five provided you several different ways a few Christians experienced God's love and intervention in their lives. Some of the testimonies involved suffering and tragedy. But each person came through their trial with a greater appreciation of God and His love for having the experience.

To Grow in Faith is to Grow in God's Love

Faith is like a muscle that is strengthened by opposition. In this world, we cannot avoid pain and suffering. But with faith in Jesus, confident we are *in* God's love and care, we have a unique ability to overcome trials and tribulation from a position of victory. Jesus has already paid the complete price—our victory is assured.

I have suffered a great deal in my life. Some of that suffering is revealed in my books, some I share when I travel and speak. And each time I tell my stories, I am immediately connected with the hearts of those learning about my trials, and how I overcame and was victorious by persevering *faith*. Pain and suffering are great equalizers of people—everyone experiences them at varying levels and times in their life.

False accusations, betrayal, and rejection are paramount on the list of my most painful sufferings. I have experienced these more than once in my life from people I would never have believed would harm me in *any* way. To this day, my heart is still mending over rejection from two people. In both cases, the moment I realized what they'd done, I crumpled to the floor, unable to remain upright under the weight of the pain. I experienced uncontrollable tears and the greatest anguish of heart I'd ever known. I cried out to God, who immediately embraced me with a rush of His love. I experienced what the Scriptures say. God was going through my pain and suffering with me. I was comforted by the Holy Spirit. And knowing Jesus had personally been falsely accused, betrayed, and rejected, I was consoled with the realization God *experientially* knows my pain.

Overcoming by God's Love

From Scripture, I found hope even my pain and suffering will be used by God for good. Romans 8:28-31 states:

> And we know that for those who love God all things work together for good, for those who are the called according to his purpose. For those whom he foreknew he also predestinated to be conformed to the image of his Son, in order that he might be the firstborn among many brothers. And those whom he predestinated he also called, and those whom he called he also justified, and those whom he justified, he also glorified. What shall we say to these things? If God be for us, who can be against us?[2]

Overcoming pain and suffering is a process that requires we remain focused on the truth of God's Word. Overcoming requires we love others as Christ loves us and that we forgive others as we have been forgiven.

Over time with the Lord's counsel, I had to admit I put too much faith in these two people. People will always let us down. I've certainly let many people down in my lifetime, which I deeply regret. But God will never let us down.

The apostle Paul wrote in Romans 5:1-8:

> Therefore, since we have been justified by faith, we have peace with God through our Lord Jesus Christ. Through

him we have also obtained access by faith into this grace in which we stand, and we rejoice in hope of the glory of God. Not only that, but we rejoice in our sufferings, knowing that suffering produces endurance, and endurance produces character, and character produces hope, and hope does not put us to shame, because God's love has been poured into our hearts through the Holy Spirit who has been given to us.

For while we were still weak, at the right time Christ died for the ungodly. For one will scarcely die for a righteous person—though perhaps for a good person one would dare even to die—but God shows his love for us in that while we were still sinners, Christ died for us.[3]

When Christ hung on the cross, unimaginably suffering unimaginable death by crucifixion at the hands of the very ones He came to save, one of His last requests of God was, "Father, forgive them, for they know not what they do" Luke 23:34.

When we suffer pain at the hands of others, and we're able to extend God's love and forgiveness toward them even if only in our hearts and minds, we have evidence God's love dwells within us. When more Christians mature to this point, and when God's love is the rule of their hearts, we will see the revolution in this world we long to see.

How to Experience God's Love

John Piper offers his comments on Romans 5:1-8 (emphasis added):
God's love poured into your heart is not the same as God's love proven to your mind. God's love poured into your

heart is a real heart-experience of being loved by God. God's love proven to your mind is the conclusion of an argument, with or without the sweetness of *feeling* loved by God in the heart. I want you to know this sweetness. I want you to enjoy this gift: the outpouring of the love of God in your hearts.

You can know in your head some things from *argument* that you don't experience in your heart from God's Spirit. For example, you might argue 1) The Bible says, "For God so loved the world" (John 3:16); 2) I am part of the world; 3) therefore, God loves me. That's one way of knowing you are loved by God.

Or you might go further and say, 1) Christ told his disciples, "Greater love has no one than this, that one lay down his life for his friends" (John 15:13); 2) I am one of his friends because I follow him and keep his commandments (John 15:14); 3) therefore Christ loves me with the greatest love.

That is a way of knowing in your head that you are loved. But that is not what Romans 5:5 is talking about. Romans 5:5 says, "Hope does not put us to shame, because God's love has been poured into our hearts through the Holy Spirit who has been given to us." This is a Spirit-given *experience* of God's love, not a logical inference from an argument. *It is something poured out.* It is something felt in the heart. Known in the way the heart knows.[4]

Piper goes on to bring out four specific aspects of what the apostle Paul wrote in Romans 5:1-8, summarized below. The endnotes provide you with the web address where you can read the entire article. Here is a summary of John Piper's points:

1. **This experience of God's love is poured out through the Holy Spirit.** Experiencing God's love is supernatural. It is not finally in our power. It is owing only to the Holy Spirit. There is something deeply wrong when we have become so naturalistic and so psychologized that we think a person with a traumatic, abusive background cannot know the love of God experientially. The authentic experience of feeling loved by God is a work of God, not a work of being well adjusted, in solid families. [The love of God] is given to us *supernaturally*, [requiring no] pedigree.

2. **This experience of God's love has factual, objective content.** God's love is poured out in our hearts. And in verse 8 it is *shown* to us. Now think about this: Is the love of God *shown to us historically* in the death of Christ for us to study and think about and know as objective fact? Or is the love of God *poured out in our hearts experientially* by the Holy Spirit? And, of course, the answer is that Paul will not let us choose between these. [Like truth and love, they are two sides of the same coin.] I say, *the Holy Spirit takes the historical facts of the Christ's death and opens the eyes of our heart to see the all-satisfying divine beauty of the love of God in it.* And thus *by the spiritual sight of God's love in the work of Christ, he pours that love into our hearts.*

3. **God's love is experienced by all Christians in some measure.** The reason I say [this is simply because of the] "our" and "us." Then notice what he says in verse 9b: "If anyone does not have the Spirit of Christ, he does not belong to Him." That means that *all Christians have the Spirit of Christ, the Holy Spirit.*
   So I conclude that all true Christians have at least tasted the outpouring of God's love in our hearts. Every true Christian knows

the love of God not just as an argument, but as an experience. That is what it means to become a Christian.

4. **The experience varies from time to time and person to person, and can be (and should be) pursued in ever fuller measures.** Consider [what the apostle Paul wrote in] 2 Thessalonians 3:5, "*May the Lord direct your hearts into the love of God and into the steadfastness of Christ.*" What does [the apostle Paul] want God to do? He wants God to "direct their hearts." This is a remarkable phrase! The heart has directions. It moves toward one thing or another. When the heart moves toward something it moves toward what it regards as attractive and satisfying and valuable. So Paul is praying that God would give the heart a sight of the love of God as more attractive and satisfying and valuable than ordinary earthly things. "May the Lord direct your hearts into the love of God." What would this be other than an experience of God's love? Paul prays for it to happen. Which means this experience can rise and fall. It can be greater or lesser. And the great desire is, O let it be greater!

God will not let you down. He will not let your hope prove empty. He won't let you be put to shame. To that end, He pours His love into your hearts by the Holy Spirit. He gives you a real, authentic experience of His love, not just an argument for His love, but an experience![5]

Our aim is to experience God's love. Once we experience the outpouring of God's love *in* us, we can help others experience it *through* us.

God's Love Uniquely Satisfies

Human love, in and of itself, will never satisfy. That's because we were created to be loved by God. Human love is need love, whereas God's love is gift love. While we enjoy human love and find some measure of fulfillment from human love, that love is not wholly satisfying.

We find comfort in the love from our parents. We experience validation in the love of our friends. We find a measure of worth from the love of a spouse. But even with all these expressions of love in place in the healthiest of ways, there is still the awareness something is missing. God created us with a yearning for His love. Until we find His love, nothing else will satisfy.

We don't have to look too far to see people who do not know God—who are looking for love in all the wrong places. You may know someone the description fits, or you may have been on a quest to satisfy your deep inner longing. That certainly described me. Because my family of origin was radically dysfunctional (my father abandoned my sister, mother and me), I thought what I needed was to hurry up and grow up and establish a close, loving family of my own to satisfy my heartache.

When I became old enough to date, I was on a mission to find the right man to marry—convinced that once I did, I would finally have all my angst resolved. From sixteen to twenty-nine years of age, I searched to find the love I thought I needed. What I found instead was the added pain of the breakup of four different relationships. When the breakup of the relationship with David occurred, the one man of all I thought I'd marry, I was utterly broken.

I don't know how I managed to see through the tears to drive home that day. When I arrived, I stumbled over to the couch where I collapsed. The tears streaming down my face were lava-hot, and the sobs came from a depth of my being I'd never experienced. My thoughts were all over the place. Questions riddled my mind.

I don't know how long I'd been on the couch when I began thinking about God. I'd heard about God from the Sunday school teacher when I attended church with our neighbors. I'm certain my mother wanted my sister and me to go to church so we would be out of the house, keeping it quiet for our father who was sleeping off the drunk from the night before.

I remembered she shared God was good and loving and wanted to help us in life. The next thing I knew, I found myself praying. "God, Jesus, Heavenly Father, if you really are the good and loving God the Sunday school teacher told me about, if you really want to help me make something good out of my life, then I need you now more than ever. I know I said a prayer as a little girl asking Jesus to come into my heart to be my forever friend. I recall praying for Jesus to be my Savior and Lord. But I haven't wanted you to be Lord. I only wanted you to be my Savior to keep me from going to hell. I've lived all these years as Lord of my own life. But, if you can truly take my life and make something good of it, I need you to, because up 'til now I've only proven all I can do is make a mess of it."

And the very moment I uttered my last syllable, I heard the voice of God speak to me. Not audibly, but Spirit to spirit. And this is what I heard God say to me in a most compassionate and loving voice:

"Pamela, you only understand in part. I brought David into your life and also took him out of your life to confirm to you it is not an earthly relationship you deeply long for—you long for Me. You met me once a long time ago. Don't you remember? You were very little. You learned about me from that Sunday school your parents let you attend with the neighbors. Remember? I promised you I would never leave or forsake you. I know you remember. You gave yourself to me then. But through the years, My heart has repeatedly been torn because you have sought the love you need in many other ways—career, position, material possessions, relationships. Yet, I have kept my promise. Though you have never acknowledged me in your heart of hearts—you only see me as Savior for your eternal future, I AM the God of yesterday, today, and tomorrow. Now, Pamela, I will wait no longer. Today, I have removed from you that which you perceive to be what you deeply long for so you can finally and abruptly see the truth about who and what you really need."

I was completely taken aback. I hadn't noticed as I heard God speak, my tears and deep sobs had stopped. I sat stunned in the dark and in silence. Then finally, I spoke aloud. "God, I now realize for the first time, I've never given my whole heart to You. I am so sorry. Today, I want You to be my Lord and Savior. I thank You for Jesus and receive Him completely today. I've tried living my life my way, and now I'm beyond ready to live it Your way."

From that moment on, my life has never been the same—neither did I ever once have the desire to return to my former ways. I experienced God's love the moment I genuinely sought Him, and I can testify only God's love will satisfy the deep inner longing of the human soul.

God's Kind of Love

God's kind of love is different than human love, not only because His love is gift love, but because His love is an unconditional *commitment*. Dr. Charles Stanley, the founder of In Touch Ministries and a *New York Times* bestselling author, defined God's love in his sermon "Starved for Love":

> God's love is a commitment to the satisfaction, security
> and development of the one loved, and a commitment to
> the fulfillment of their needs, whatever they are, always
> asking what is best for the object of the love.[6]

In most human relationships today, commitment is sorely lacking. When our culture revered God and considered marriage as holy and unto God, the traditional wedding vows exchanged were a declaration of commitment unto death. One such sample of traditional marriage vows follows:

MALE

I ______, take you _______, to be my lawfully wedded wife. To have and to hold, from this day forward, for better, for worse, for richer, for poorer, in sickness or in health, to love and to cherish till death do us part. And hereto I pledge you my faithfulness.

FEMALE

I, ______, take you _______, to be my lawfully wedded husband. To have and to hold, from this day forward, for better, for worse, for richer, for poorer, in sickness and in health, to love and to cherish, till death do us part. And hereto I pledge you my faithfulness.

We rarely hear wedding vows today reflecting the values stated above. Neither do we see many marriages stand the test of life's adversities as they once did. I venture to say this is because God is not recognized or revered as He once was. Also, only people who have chosen to receive God's love are capable of giving love. Most of what we see as love in our culture today is human love with all its failures.

God's kind of love brings a host of benefits. Here are nine, although there are many more. God's love:

1. Brings healing.
2. Provides a strong sense of self-worth.
3. Produces a confident feeling of emotional completeness.
4. Gives complete security.

5. Helps us to love those who have wronged us.

6. Equips us to be kind toward those who have misunderstood or misjudged us.

7. Empowers us to serve others joyfully, even sacrificially.

8. Enables us to develop a spiritually intimate relationship with Him, and allows for better intimate human relationships.

9. Compels us to share God's love with other people.

Spotting people who are outside God's love isn't difficult. Many are restless, dissatisfied, lonely, angry. Driven to satisfy the God-given need to be loved, not knowing only God's love satisfies, many engage in immoral sexual involvements with some even willing to try to buy love.

God's plan is once we discover His truly amazing, unconditional and eternal love, we help others discover His love. We get to play a part in God's plan of bringing all who belong to Him into the family of God. For us to do this well, we need to better understand God's love. The next two sections are intended to help.

Many Expressions of God's Love

Beyond God's supreme expression of His love through the life, death, and resurrection of Jesus, God is continually revealing His love for you. Searching Scripture and learning how God has intervened in the lives of His people since the beginning of time reveals His love is continually expressed in countless ways. We can never exhaust God's love.

Linda Sommer's article, "Four Ways God Shows His Love for Us" provides an overview of four compelling ways God's love toward us is expressed:

Grace–The height of God's love is grace. His grace is poured out upon you from above.

Forgiveness–The depth of God's love is forgiveness. His forgiveness goes deep within the recesses of your soul and cleanses and restores you.

Truth–The breadth of God's love is His truth. God's truth is able to set you free to walk in all the fullness of His love. His truth is able to expand your mind so you can experience His boundless love.

Mercy–The length of God's love is His mercy. His mercy extends forever and ever to every generation.[7]

Scripture reveals God's love is expressed in many different ways that provide distinct benefits. Here are seven specific ways God's love lavishly provides benefit to us.

1. **God loves us with Atoning love.** "For God so loved the world that he gave his only Son, that whoever believes in him should not perish but have eternal life" (John 3:16). We cannot consider deeply enough that God's love for us motivated Jesus to personally come into the world to save us. His sacrifice not only brings us peace with God but also brings us into a personal, loving relationship with Him. God's atoning love through Christ is the source of all our spiritual blessings (see Romans 5:1-5).

2. **God loves us with a Calling love.** "But you are a chosen race, a royal priesthood, a holy nation, a people for his own possession, that you may proclaim the excellencies of him who called you out of darkness and into his marvelous light" (1 Peter 2:9). God's love calls us out of the darkness of sin and into the light of fellowship with Him. And because He has called us to Himself, He promises

to protect our relationship with Him and never leave or forsake us. (See John 10:28, Hebrews 13:5 and 1Thessalonians 5:23-25).

3. **God loves us with Redeeming love.** "For God has done what the law, weakened by the flesh, could not do. By sending his own Son in the likeness of sinful flesh and for sin, he condemned sin in the flesh, in order that the righteous requirement of the law might be fulfilled in us, who walk not according to the flesh but according to the Spirit" (Romans 8:3-4). Because we are born at enmity with God by inherited sin, we have no power to fulfill God's law. God's love shown through Christ who fulfilled the law for us, and redeemed us out of rebellion (see Galatians 3:13).

4. **God loves us with Justifying love.** "For all have sinned and fall short of the glory of God, and are justified by his grace as a gift, through the redemption that is in Christ Jesus, whom God put forward as a propitiation [atonement] by his blood, to be received by faith" (Romans 3:23-25) [added words mine]. When we place our faith in Christ, we are immediately justified, or considered innocent, by God's grace in Christ. God now sees us through Christ's righteousness instead of through our sin.

5. **God loves us with Adopting love.** "For you did not receive the spirit of slavery to fall back into fear, but you have received the Spirit of adoption as sons, by whom we cry Abba [Father in Aramaic] Father!"(Romans 8:15). God not only forgives our sin but goes even further by adopting us into His family. Faith in Jesus qualifies us to share in Christ's inheritance along with all the saints. (See Colossians 1:12) This inheritance includes additional demonstrations of God's love including, salvation, strength, hope, peace, comfort, providence, fellowship, and much more!

6. **God loves us with Sanctifying love.** "… we have been sanctified through the offering of the body of Jesus Christ once for all" (Hebrews 10:10). Sanctifying us means God has set us apart for His purpose. We're sanctified in two ways: *positionally* and *progressively*. We're sanctified positionally when we come to Christ. Since we are no longer at enmity with God, we are repositioned into the family of God. We're sanctified progressively, as we cooperate with the Holy Spirit to continually be conformed more and more into the image of Christ.

7. **God loves us with Glorifying love.** "See what kind of love the Father has given to us, that we should be called children of God; and so we are. The reason why the world does not know us is that it did not know him. Beloved, we are God's children now, and what we will be has not yet appeared; but we know that when he appears we shall be like him, because we shall see him as he is," (1 John 3:1-2). Throughout our lives, we will struggle with sin, but by God's sanctifying love and His promise to see the good work He began in us to completion, we will prevail. When we go to be with the Lord, we will be like Him and remain with Him forever. God's glorifying love is the ultimate destination for Christians (see Philippians 1:6).

Next, we'll consider specifically how we can be an extension of God's love and radically change the world, one person at a time.

CHAPTER TWELVE

Being an Extension of God's Love

Once you've entered into God's love, you are spiritually transformed into an entirely new creature *and* you are given a place in God's ministry of reconciliation. We read in 2 Corinthians 5:17-20a:

> … if anyone is in Christ, he is a new creation. The old has passed away; behold, the new has come. All this is from God, who through Christ reconciled us to himself and gave us the ministry of reconciliation; that is, in Christ God was reconciling the world to himself, not counting their trespasses against them, and entrusting to us the message of reconciliation. Therefore, we are ambassadors for Christ, God making his appeal through us.

Everyone who is a genuine believer in Jesus as their Lord and Savior not only gets the incredible blessing of being reconciled to God but also gets to become an extension of God's love. This ministry of reconciliation allows us to share God's love from the overflow of our heart. What inexpressible joy to be able to demonstrate our gratitude to God for saving us by serving

Him. And why wouldn't we want to devote ourselves to sharing God's love, finally knowing God's love is what the world desperately needs? He is what we desperately needed and what we have been abundantly blessed to find.

When we read a good book, experience a great restaurant, or watch a great movie, we naturally share the experience with others. Since entering the love of God means eternal joy, peace, freedom, and the greatest sense of belonging we could ever hope to have God's love is the greatest experience we can share. Luke 11:33 reads, "No one after lighting a lamp puts it in a cellar or under a basket, but on a stand, so that those who enter may see the light."

God worked many situations and circumstances in your life to bring you to discover Him and His love. He intends you to be more than a light on a light stand. He intends you to be a beacon on a hill. You will want to spend time in your new-found faith to learn more about God and His perfect instructions to enable you to live your new life in the fullness of His promises. Finding a mentor, finding a good church, and getting involved in Bible study are all excellent and essential foundation building engagements. While you are establishing your firm foundation, be prayerful to discover your specific place in God's plan.

The Way of God's Love

Nowhere in Scripture is "what God's love looks like" better explained than in 1 Corinthians chapter 13. In fact, this chapter has become known as *the Love Chapter.* To understand the love God has for us and the love we are to extend to others, we need to be well-versed in chapter 13, (emphasis added):

> If I speak in the tongues of men and of angels, but have
> not love, I am a noisy gong or a clanging cymbal. And if I

have prophetic powers, and understand all mysteries and all knowledge, and if I have all faith, so as to remove mountains, but have not love, I am nothing. If I give away all I have, and if I deliver up my body to be burned, but have not love, I gain nothing.

Love is patient and kind; love does not envy or boast; it is not arrogant or rude. It does not insist on its own way; it is not irritable or resentful; it does not rejoice at wrongdoing, but rejoices with the truth. Love bears all things, believes all things, hopes all things, endures all things.

Love never ends. As for prophecies, they will pass away; as for tongues, they will cease; as for knowledge, it will pass away. For we know in part and we prophesy in part, but *when the perfect comes*, the partial will pass away. When I was a child, I spoke like a child, I thought like a child, I reasoned like a child. When I became a man, I gave up childish ways. For now we see in a mirror dimly, but then face to face. Now I know in part; then I shall know fully, even as I have been fully known.

So now faith, hope, and love abide, these three; but the greatest of these is love.[1]

The phrase, *when the perfect comes,* is agreed by many scholars to refer to the second coming of Jesus when He will destroy all wickedness and establish His rule in a new heaven and earth. This is the point in eternity when all who belong to Christ will be transformed. The apostle Paul explains in 1 Corinthians 15:51-53:

> Behold! I tell you a mystery. We shall not all sleep, [die in our natural body] but we shall all be changed, in a moment, in the twinkling of an eye, at the last trumpet. For the trumpet will sound, and the dead will be raised imperishable, and we [those still living] shall be changed. For this perishable body must put on the imperishable, and this mortal body must put on immortality.

All believers look forward to Christ's return when the work of the cross will be complete, and the influence of sin and its source destroyed. Then, we will be fully restored and live with God in the same manner He originally intended for all humanity. This is the final expression of our hope—the same hope we are to help others discover.

Reformers Unite

You have finally discovered your true identity through faith in Christ. You have entered into the love of God and all its abundant blessings. You have a new and accurate understanding of your value and worth. You have your unique place as part of a movement that is bigger than you, alone. You are now part of God's worldwide team of reformers, who are commissioned to help others discover the real and certain hope of Jesus. You are an ambassador for Christ, with all His authority given to you!

What does it mean to be an ambassador for Christ? It means you have all His authority and power to utilize on earth. Matthew 28:18-20 tells us in His resurrected state, Jesus appeared to His disciples and commissioned them.

Generally speaking, an ambassador is a respected official acting as a representative of a nation. Sent to a foreign land, the ambassador's role is to reflect the official position of the sovereign body that gave him authority. Similarly, all of us who have placed our faith in Jesus, who is now in heaven are representatives of Him on earth. Those whose faith is in Jesus have exchanged their earthly citizenship for a heavenly citizenship. We are no longer a part of this world, even though we live here. Indeed, we represent heaven on earth, and as ambassadors, we are commissioned to make God's kingdom visible on earth. We accomplish God's will on earth through first seeking to hear Him, then knowing His will, and finally acting on His will.

We know God in a general sense through creation. We know God's will in an intellectual manner through studying the Bible, His Word. And we can know God's will in an intimate way through prayer.

Communicating with God

Prayer is our direct line to heaven. Prayer is a communication process that allows us to talk to God. He wants us to communicate with Him. God passionately encourages prayer and states He desires to make His people joyful in His house of prayer, saying His house shall be called a house of prayer for all people (Isaiah 56:7).

Many people question what prayer is because they desire to pray, but they don't know how. AllAboutGod.com is an online ministry that offers the following for understanding prayer:

> **What Do I Say?** Praying is like talking to your best friend! It's easy to talk to someone when you know they love you unconditionally! [Your very first effective prayer will be to:]
>
> 1. Ask Jesus to forgive you of your sins and make you new in Him! Now turn from your sins and turn to God so you can be cleansed of your sins (Acts 3:19).

2. Tell Him your needs! Give all your worries and cares to God, for He cares about what happens to you (1 Peter 5:7).

3. Thank Him, for He died on the cross at Calvary for us! For God so loved the world that He gave his only Son, so that everyone who believes in Him will not perish but have eternal life (John 3:16).

How Do I Say It? Here's how I have learned to approach the Savior of my life.

1. With confidence and belief that He will deliver: Because of Christ and our faith in Him, we can now come fearlessly into God's presence, assured of His glad welcome (Ephesians 3:12). So let us come boldly to the throne of our gracious God. There we will receive His mercy, and we will find grace to help us when we need it (Hebrews 4:16).

2. With joy that He can deliver. You have shown me the way of life, and You will give me wonderful joy in your presence (Acts 2:28).

3. With expectation that He is going to deliver. Listen to my voice in the morning, LORD. Each morning I bring my requests to You and wait expectantly (Psalm 5:3). I am praying to You because I know You will answer, O God. Bend down and listen as I pray (Psalm 17:6).

What is Prayer?—What Does the Bible Say?

Pray for each other. Jesus set an example for us on what to pray. He prayed for His disciples and for every generation to come that would follow Him. His prayer was that God protect and strengthen them as long as they were in this world. Jesus also prayed for those who would come to believe in Him through the Gospel message (John 17).

Pray with faith. So, you see, it is impossible to please God without faith. Anyone who wants to come to Him must believe that there is a God and that He rewards those who sincerely seek Him (Hebrews 11:6).

Pray with worship and reverence. Exalt the LORD our God! Bow low before His feet, for He is holy! (Psalm 99:5). Yes, Lord, the man said, I believe! And he worshiped Jesus (John 9:38). You will know with confidence that God can hear you when you pray, so open that line of communication! Pray, knowing that no matter how far you roam, your connection with Him can never be lost! I pray that your love for each other will overflow more and more, and that you will keep on growing in your knowledge and understanding (Philippians 1:9).[2]

God's Will Be Done on Earth

When one of Jesus' disciples asked Him to teach them to pray, Jesus responded (Matthew 6:5-13):

When you pray, you must not be like the hypocrites. For they love to stand and pray in the synagogues and at the street corners, that they may be seen by others. Truly, I say to you, they have received their reward. But when you pray, go into your room and shut the door and pray to your Father who is in secret. And your Father who sees in secret will reward you.

And when you pray, do not heap up empty phrases as the Gentiles do, for they think that they will be heard for their many words. Do not be like them, for your Father knows what you need before you ask him. Pray then like this:

'Our Father in heaven, hallowed be your name. Your kingdom come, your will be done, on earth as it is in heaven. Give us this day our daily bread, and forgive us our debts, as we also have forgiven our debtors. And lead us not into temptation, but deliver us from evil.'[3]

Jesus was very clear with His teaching that prayer to God should be simple and from a pure and humble heart to communicate with God—not to impress people.

Jesus provided that model prayer often referred to as *the Lord's Prayer.*

Opening the prayer with *Our Father* conveys the authority, warmth, and intimacy of a loving father's care. The term *Our Father* also denotes believers are all part of one family with God as the head.

In heaven reminds us of God's sovereign rule over all things.

Hallowed be Your name proclaims we recognize and accept God's name is to be revered, and God will be treated with the highest honor and set apart as holy.

Your kingdom come is a statement of agreeing with God that Christians are called to pray and work for the continual advancement of God's kingdom on earth. The presence of God's kingdom in this age refers to the reign of

Christ in the hearts and lives of believers and in the church at large. We advance God's kingdom on earth by reflecting His love, obeying His commandments, honoring Him, doing good for all people, and proclaiming the good news of the gospel.

Your will be done on earth as it is in heaven expresses submission to God's will and acknowledgment that just as God's will is perfectly done in heaven, we're to pray His will be evident the same way here on earth.

Give us this day our daily bread acknowledges dependence on God for our basic necessity of life which by implication includes all of the believer's daily physical needs.

Forgive us our debts as we forgive our debtors, is a request for the restoration of fellowship with God when fellowship has been hindered by sin. This petition also acknowledges the one praying seeks to be as forgiving of others as God has been forgiving of them. In Matthew 6:14-15, Jesus stated, "For if you forgive others their trespasses, your heavenly Father will also forgive you, but if you do not forgive others their trespasses, neither will your Father forgive your trespasses." God's holy love motivates Him to forgive us. The evidence we are in God's love is revealed by the way we forgive those who offend us.

Lead us not into temptation is asking to be spared from difficult circumstances that would tempt us to sin. God never directly tempts believers, although He does sometimes lead us into situations to test us. Remember testing our faith is an opportunity to strengthen our faith. Testing is not God's effort to defeat us, but to strengthen us to contend against the evil one, namely Satan.

Deliver us from evil acknowledges God as our Deliverer/Redeemer/Savior. The word translated "evil" can mean either evil or the evil one.

When the Lord's Prayer is recited, the concluding words are often, "For Yours is the kingdom, and the power, and the glory forever. Amen." The most reliable and oldest Greek manuscripts lack these words. They are believed to have been a later scribal addition, and for that reason, they are not included in many translations of the Bible. However, there is nothing theologically incorrect about the wording, and it is not inappropriate to include them in public prayers. I personally like the closing words as they reveal complete submission to, dependence on, and, worship of God. The word *Amen* basically means "so be it."

Position of Prayer

You'll read about many postures people take in prayer—standing, rocking, kneeling, prostrate on the floor, hands lifted, head bowed, with eyes open, with eyes closed. You may pray aloud, you may pray in your heart, you may journal your prayers. You may pray in the Spirit or in the natural man. The posture you take when you pray will be between you and God and will likely take on different forms depending on the setting.

Regardless of the posture, always remember the position. You are not praying from the position of an orphan. You are not praying as a widow/widower. You are not praying from the position of poverty. You are not praying from a position of rejection. You are not praying from a positon of fear. You are not praying from the position of sickness, disease or death. NO! Jesus has overcome all these things and more. You must never pray from the position of victim and must always pray from the position of a victor.

Effective prayers are prayers expecting God to make good on all His promises without Him being a respecter of persons or partial in any way. Effective prayers are prayers that pray God's own words back to Him with the belief and expectation God is good for His Word. Effective prayers are what move God to produce results. And with faith the size of a mustard seed, your prayers can move mountains, according to the very words of Jesus (see Matthew 17:20).

I don't believe in the doctrine known as the *Faith Word* or *Word of Faith*, or *Name It, Claim It* movement. We don't identify what we want and then tell God on what He is to do for us. We are to find out what He says He will do and get in position to receive those things.

Listening to God

A good number of professing Christians fail to have a vibrant prayer life for many reasons. However, perhaps the most common reason is they only pray to God— they don't listen for His response. Imagine if your spouse or loved one only talked to you and never listened to hear anything you said. There's no relationship in that—that's a monolog. If Christians pray in monolog style, they have no exchange of relationship with God through prayer, which greatly limits their effective life in Christ.

Jesus Himself said He always listened to the Father, and He only spoke what the Father revealed, and only did what the Father instructed Him to do.

He is our example. Jesus listened to and obeyed the Father with a heart of submission and awareness that the Father's mission was His mission and purpose. Jesus suffered all He did in His human life solely motived by God's love for us. We then, ought to follow His example to listen and obey, to wholly enter into God's plan and purpose with a heart of gratitude that we have been saved and set apart for good works. Our mandate is to expand God's kingdom, so His will is done. Imagine the positive impact on the world if more of us learned the discipline of hearing God and obeying His voice. I explored this concept in greater detail in *Renew Your Hope!*

Remedy for Personal Breakthroughs. You can find more help there. For now, I want to explore some of the ways the Lord speaks to us.

Hearing God

God speaks to all of us in many different ways. I'm convinced He selects the way(s) based on our personality, level of faith, maturity, and knowledge. We must never envy other believers because of the interactive relationship they have. God relates to each of us uniquely. When we find ourselves wanting more than what we have in terms of our relationship with God, all we need do is ask Him for more. Scripture states when we ask for things consistent with His revealed will and do not doubt, God hears us and answers our prayers (see 1 John 5:14 and James 1:5-8). Below are some ways God speaks to believers along with very brief overview descriptions. There's so much more you can learn if you desire.

- **Through His Living**—Jesus is referred to as *God's Word made flesh*, making Him the embodiment of God's promises. He is also referred to as *the Living Word*. Revealing the reality of Jesus to a person whose heart is ripe is one very special way God not only talks to us but connects us to Himself.

- **Through His Written Word**—The Bible is another special gift to us, allowing us to read about God's loving and faithful intervention in the lives of humans. Everything we need to learn about the character, will, and intentions of God for humanity and how we can access the very best God has for us are contained in the pages of the Bible.

- **Through His Spoken Word**—God's spoken word can be a still small voice you hear in your heart-mind, or a truth uttered by another individual that resonates with you and is confirmed by the inner witness of the Holy Spirit.

- **Through His Holy Spirit**—The Holy Spirit, given us by God, is our Teacher, Counselor, Comforter and more. He uses a variety of different ways to get our attention including a sense of danger, elation, "knowing," or a physical response to His witness such as "Holy Ghost bumps."

- **Through Creation**—All of creation awaits the full redemption God has planned in the fullness of time. Creation not only attests to the existence and beauty of God but also reveals the blessings and judgments of God.

- **Through Circumstances**—God is ever at work to engineer situations and circumstances to guide and direct us and to get our attention. Nothing that happens in life is a coincidence. All is done under the watchful eye of God.

- **Through Others**—God can zap anything into existence any time He wants, but most often He works through people. A person may have an experience they relate that confirms a direction for you, they may have a word of knowledge or prophecy, they may be the messenger or conduit of a material blessing or loving admonition.

- **Through Arts**—Music, poetry, paintings and other mediums of art are often used by God to reach the souls of men. The arts provide a way of connecting to our souls that bypasses the intellect and connects with emotions.

- **Through Prayer**—Prayer is the intimate communion with God that enjoins, renews and uplifts our spirit. Prayer is a powerful offensive weapon for believers that brings God's kingdom to earth.

- **Through Peace**—God will occasionally provide reassurance by imparting a supernatural peace. A supernatural peace is an encompassing feeling that isn't logical given the natural realities. God also gives peace at times of being perplexed, perhaps when needing to make a decision, that directs us in the matter.

- **Through Discomfort**—When we get complacent or we have veered off the path He's determined for us, God often uses discomfort to get us back on track.

- **Through Supernatural Means**—Both the Old and New Testaments reveal many times God supernaturally manifested a matter as a demonstration and/or confirmation.

- **Through Impressions**—You may experience a sense that does not engage your mind but may be experienced as a feeling or as a visual image in your being.

- **Through Dreams and Visions**—God speaks to believers through night dreams and waking visions.

- **Any other way He wants**—The Old Testament reveals God speaking through a rainbow, through a burning bush, through plagues, through a whirlwind, even through a donkey. The New Testament records all manner of signs and wonders provided as means of provision and confirmation.

Before you conclude a matter is a word from God for you, you must confirm what you think you hear does not run contrary to the written Word of God. God will never violate His written Word. Part of the reason He's given us the Bible is so we have a means of confirming the source of the voices or messages we receive. God's direction will always be life-affirming, with love and encouragement. Any messages that evoke a sense of condemnation, fear, dread, anxiety, hate, division, jealousy, and the like, are not from God!

Dress for Success

You're part of a growing reformation movement. Like any movement for change, there will be opposition. God is not caught off-guard, and He has already provided us the armor and equipment we need. The apostle Paul wrote to believers in Ephesus from a jail cell, clearly maintaining the position of the victor. He instructs believers to this day:

> Finally, be strong in the Lord and in the strength of his might. Put on the whole armor of God, that you may be able to stand against the schemes of the devil. For we do not wrestle against flesh and blood, but against the rulers, against the authorities, against the cosmic powers over this present darkness, against the spiritual forces of evil in the heavenly places. Therefore take up the whole armor of God, that you may be able to withstand in the evil day, and having done all, to stand firm. Stand therefore, having fastened on the belt of truth, and having put on the breastplate of righteousness, and, as shoes for your feet, having put on the readiness given by the gospel of peace. In all circumstances take up the shield of faith, with which you can extinguish all the flaming darts of the evil one; and take the helmet of salvation, and the sword of the Spirit, which is the Word of God, praying at all times in the Spirit, with all prayer and supplication. To that end, keep alert with all perseverance, making supplication for all the saints, and also for me, that words may be given to me in opening

> my mouth boldly to proclaim the mystery of the gospel, for
> which I am an ambassador in chains, that I may declare it
> boldly, as I ought to speak.[4]

This reformation—this radical demonstration of God's love—is exactly what this anxious world of unrest needs. Our real enemy is the devil and his evil followers. God wants Christians to be known by our love. We're to be known by our love for God, our love for one another, and our love for humanity.

We must keep forefront in our minds our battle is not against people. Our battle is a spiritual battle. Ephesians 6:12 clearly states, "For we do not wrestle against flesh and blood, but against the rulers, against the authorities, against the cosmic powers over this present darkness, against the spiritual forces of evil in the heavenly places." This one truth—that our fight is not against people—must be heralded. Our real enemy is the devil and his evil followers.

The world has been in a spiritual battle since Satan first enticed Adam and Eve to reject God and choose their own way. While they thought they were choosing their own way, in reality, they were beguiled by the enemy and unwittingly chose Satan's way.

To this day, there are thousands of people who are deceived by the enemy and truly under his influence and control. They don't know they are because, again, that is the nature of deception—the victim is unaware. Just as we didn't break free from our natural-born state of enmity with God until the love of God reached down into our hearts, neither will they. Jesus died for every single human being who will respond to God's love, and place their faith in Him.

People who are under Satan's influence and control will say and do things that bring the people of God harm because the enemy wants to destroy all that belongs to God. That includes us. When people do things to harm us and act like our enemies, we are to love them. Jesus was spit at in the face, reviled, falsely accused, beaten, and crucified. Yet, He remained motived by the Father's love and expressed nothing but love to those who were persecuting Him.

Loving our "enemies" or the people who are pawns to Satan's wiles is like heaping hot coals on the evil demons' heads. Love infuriates the enemy because he is not getting the reaction of hatred and destruction he seeks. We are to love the people but hate the spiritual enemy who is influencing them. Don't think there are "neutral" people. There are not. People are either an enemy of God under the influence of Satan, or they are saved by Jesus with the choice to be on God's team of reformers.

Those of us who have been blessed to discover truth are to share the good news—the gospel message of Jesus and God's amazing love.

Radical Reformation Revival

The pop-culture band, the Beatles, were onto something when they sang, "All we need is love." Could it be forty years ago God wanted to do a radical reformation revival? I think so. Because at the same time the Beatles and the Hippie Movement promoted "love power," the Jesus Movement came on the scene. There was great momentum promoting love.

I believe the enemy of God went into high gear to overturn any good that could have come from the movements. In the four or so decades since the popularity of the Beatles' lyrics, we've seen a steady increase of immorality, drug abuse, power abuse, corrupt leadership, dissolution of families, and destruction and death of all sorts. We need to recognize these for what they are—the works of the enemy who seeks only to lie, rob, kill, and destroy. Perhaps now, as we have gone through suffering, God has gained our attention through the "discomfort."

Forty years is a time of completion. After God had freed the Old Testament Israelites from slavery in Egypt, they wandered in the desert until the "opposition from within the camp," died off. Israelite spies who went ahead to see if there was any opposition in the land God promised to them, returned with fearful reports of giants in the land. But, Joshua and Caleb, who represented the next generation, knew God was for them, so their victory was certain. Then, Joshua and Caleb were in a position to take hold of the fullness of God's promise.

God's people—those who are truly led by His Spirit—have the ability to bring about a radical reformation revival today. It's not a job for the half-hearted. Only those who are fully sold-out to God can accomplish His will. Jesus said in Matthew 12:30, "Whoever is not with me is against me, and whoever does not gather with me scatters." It's not going to be easy. But nothing of any worth ever is.

Where are you in this much-needed radical reformation revival? All we need is love—God's love. And we who know His love are in perfect position. We can be the reformers to produce what's in our God-filled hearts to change our lives and the world for the better. Amen.

1 John 5:1-5

Everyone who believes that Jesus is the Christ has been born of God, and everyone who loves the Father loves whoever has been born of him. By this we know that we love the children of God, when we love God and obey his commandments. For this is the love of God, that we keep his commandments. And his commandments are not burdensome. For everyone who has been born of God overcomes the world. And this is the victory that has overcome the world—our faith. Who is it that overcomes the world except the one who believes that Jesus is the Son of God?

CHAPTER ENDNOTES

Chapter One

1. *Proof that God Exists*, December 2016,
http://www.proofthatgodexists.org/quotes/, 2/10/2017.
2. *What is the best evidence argument for intelligent design?* Got Questions?
https://gotquestions.org/evidence-intelligent-design.html, 2/10/2017.
3. *What is cultural relativism?* April 2017,
https://www.gotquestions.org/cultural-relativism.html, 3/5/3017.
4. Richard L. Strauss, "God is Love," *The Joy of Knowing God* series;
https://bible.org/seriespage/14-god-love, 2/10/2017.

Chapter Two

1. Dan Harris, "Americans Surprisingly Flexible about Religion and Faith,"
ABC News with Diane Sawyer (December 2009), November 8, 2016,
http://abcnews.go.com/WN/pew-study-finds-americans-surprisingly-
flexible-faith-religion/story?id=9306080, 2/10/2017.
2. Dr. Alice von Hildebrand, *The Secular War on the Supernatural* (Essay
delivered on June 13, 1998), https://www.romancatholicman.com/secular-
war-supernatural-alice-von-hildebrand/, 10/29/2016.
3. "How Millennials Compare to their Grandparents 50 Years Ago," *Pew
Research Center*, (March 19, 2015), *Fact Tank News in the Numbers*,
http://www.pewresearch.org/fact-tank/2015/03/19/how-millennials-
compare-with-their-grandparents/, 2/14/2017.
4. Melanie Curtin, "Why Millennials Should Stop Trying to Be
Successful...Immediately," Inc.com, http://www.inc.com/melanie-
curtin/why-millennials-feel-more-pressure-to-succeed-than-any-other-
generation.html, 2/14/2017.
5. *Suicide in France*, Wikipedia,
https://en.wikipedia.org/wiki/Suicide_in_France, February 14, 2017.
6. Lynne Hinton, "Understanding, and Acting Upon, One of Our Most
Basic Desires," *The Charlotte Observer*, July 28, 2016,
http://www.charlotteobserver.com/living/religion/article92327002.html,
10/29/2016.
7. *Theological Liberalism*, October 28, 2016,
http://www.theopedia.com/theological-liberalism, 3/1/2017.
8. *The ESV Study Bible*®, ESV® Bible, Copyright 2008 by Crossway. The
Holy Bible, English Standard Version® (ESV®) Copyright © 2001 by
Crossway, a publishing ministry of Good News Publishers, ESV Text

Edition: 2011, *The Bible In Christianity,* 2619.
9. *Ibid.*
10. *Christianity,* "Where does the concept of a God-shaped hole originate?," November 5, 2016, http://christianity.stackexchange.com/questions/2746/where-does-the-concept-of-a-god-shaped-hole-originate, 3/1/2017.
11. Saul McLeod, *Maslow's Hierarchy of Needs,* (Simply Psychology, 2007 Revised 2016) https://www.simplypsychology.org/maslow.html, 4/2/2017.
12. *Belongingness,* Wikipedia, https://en.wikipedia.org/wiki/Belongingness, 2/10/2017.

Chapter Three

1. J. I. Packer, *Knowing God* (Downers Grove, Il, *InterVarsity Press,* 1973), 117.
2. D. A. Carson, *The Difficult Doctrine of the Love of God* (Wheaton, IL, *Crossway Books,* 2000), 9-16.
3. *When Were Satan and His Angels Cast Out of Heaven?,* October 30, 2016, http://www.biblesprout.com/articles/hell/Satan-cast-heaven, 3/1/2017.
4. Erwin W. Lutzer, *Christ Among Other gods: A Defense of Christ in an Age of Tolerance* (Chicago, IL: *Moody Publishers,* 1994), 134.

Chapter Four

1. J. I. Packer, *Knowing God* (Downers Grove, Il, *Inter Varsity Press,* 1973), 124.
2 Matt Slick, *What is a Covenant,* October 31 ,2016, https://carm.org/questions-covenant, 3/1/2017.
3. *The ESV Study Bible®,* ESV® Bible, Copyright 2008 by *Crossway.* The Holy Bible, English Standard Version® (ESV®) Copyright © 2001 by Crossway, a publishing ministry of Good News Publishers, ESV Text Edition: 2011, *The Bible In Christianity,*1619 and 1622.

Chapter Five

1. *When and why was Saul's name changed to Paul?* Got Questions? https://www.gotquestions.org/Saul-Paul.html, 3/15/2017.

Chapter Six

1. John Rinehart "What God Thinks About Me?" *Desiring God,* September

24, 2015, http://www.desiringgod.org/articles/what-god-thinks-about-you, 3/1/2017.
2. *Comparative Study Bible, Revised Edition,* The Amplified Bible, Expanded Edition, (Grand Rapids, MI, *The Zondervan Corporation and the Lockman Foundation,* 1987) 286.
3. *Vine's Expository Dictionary of Biblical Words,* (Nashville, TN, *Thomas Nelson, Inc.,* 1985), 130-131.
4. J. I. Packer, *Knowing God* (Downers Grove, Il, *Inter Varsity Press,* 1973), 34.
5. "Christians More Like Jesus or Pharisees?" *Barna Research Group,* June 3, 2013, https://www.barna.com/research/christians-more-like-jesus-or-pharisees/, 2/14/2017.

Chapter Seven

1. Dr. Grant Mullen, "What Happens to the Three Parts of Man at Salvation?" http://drgrantmullen.com/q-a-forums/we-have-three-parts/, 2/16/2017.
2. *Ibid.*
3. *The ESV Study Bible®,* ESV® Bible, Copyright 2008 by *Crossway.* The Holy Bible, English Standard Version® (ESV®) Copyright © 2001 by Crossway, a publishing ministry of Good News Publishers, ESV Text Edition: 2011, *The Spirit's Work in God's People,* 2521.
4. Rick Ezell, "Sermon: Knowing God Loves Me–Psalm 103," http://www.lifeway.com/Article/sermon-knowing-god-loves-me-psalm-103, 2/15/2017.

Chapter Eight

1. C. S. Lewis, *Mere Christianity,* (New York, N.Y. *Macmillan Publishing Company,* 1952), 120.
2. Billy Graham, "The Three Invitations of Christ," May 2, 2012, *Decision Magazine,* https://billygraham.org/decision-magazine/may-2012/the-three-invitations-of-christ/, 2/17/2017.

Chapter Nine

1. *The ESV Study Bible®,* ESV® Bible, Copyright 2008 by *Crossway.* The Holy Bible, English Standard Version® (ESV®) Copyright © 2001 by Crossway, a publishing ministry of Good News Publishers, ESV Text Edition: 2011, Romans 8:14-17, 2170-2171.
2. *Ibid.,* Revelation 19:6-9, 2491.

Chapter Ten

1. John Piper, "The Fall of Satan and the Victory of Christ," August 19, 2007 *Desiring God*, http://www.desiringgod.org/messages/the-fall-of-satan-and-the-victory-of-christ , 3/6/3017.
2. Dr. Jeff Iorg, "How to Write Your Own Personal Mission Statement," *Lifeway*, http://www.lifeway.com/Article/How-to-Write-Your-Own-Personal-Mission-Statement#author_bio_0, 3/4/2017.
3. Damian Pros, "Five Reasons Why Writing Down Goals Increases the Odds of Achieving Them," June 30, 2015, *The Elite Daily*, http://elitedaily.com/money/writing-down-your-goals/1068863/ 3/4/2017.

Chapter Eleven

1. John Piper, "How is God's Love Experienced in the Heart?" November 30, 1999, *Desiring God*, http://www.desiringgod.org/articles/how-is-gods-love-experienced-in-the-heart, 2/17/2017.
2. *The ESV Study Bible®*, ESV® Bible, Copyright 2008 by *Crossway*. The Holy Bible, English Standard Version® (ESV®) Copyright © 2001 by Crossway, a publishing ministry of Good News Publishers, ESV Text Edition: 2011, Romans 8:28-31, 2171-2172.
3. *Ibid.*, Romans 5:6-8, 2165.
4. John Piper, "How to Experience the Outpouring of God's Love," May 1, 2016, *Desiring God*, http://www.desiringgod.org/messages/how-to-experience-the-outpouring-of-god-s-love, 2/18/2017
5. *Ibid.*
6. Charles Stanley, "Starved for Love," *In Touch Ministries*, July 10, 2015, https://www.intouch.org/watch/starved-for-love-video, 2/28/2017.
7. Linda Sommer, "Four Ways God Shows His Love for Us." Charisma Magazine, November 14, 2013, http://www.charismamag.com/spirit/spiritual-growth/8334-4-ways-god-shows-his-love-for-us, 2/18/2017.

Chapter Twelve

1. *The ESV Study Bible®*, ESV® Bible, Copyright 2008 by *Crossway*. The Holy Bible, English Standard Version® (ESV®) Copyright © 2001 by Crossway, a publishing ministry of Good News Publishers, ESV Text Edition: 2011, 1 Corinthians 13, 2211.
2. "What is Prayer," *All About God*, http://www.allaboutprayer.org/what-is-prayer.htm, 2/20/2017.

3. *The ESV Study Bible*®, ESV® Bible, Copyright 2008 by *Crossway*. The Holy Bible, English Standard Version® (ESV®) Copyright © 2001 by Crossway, a publishing ministry of Good News Publishers, ESV Text Edition: 2011, Matthew 6:5-13, 1831-1832.
4. *Ibid.* Ephesians 6:10-20, 2273-2274.

About the Author

Pamela Christian's ministry began in the early 1990s serving as Teaching/Director for Community Bible Study, an independent, international organization. This was followed by invitations to speak across the country for various organizations, which she continues to enjoy with great enthusiasm to this day. Her initial writing work included the development of workbooks for her retreats and conferences. This soon expanded to publication in book compilations, magazines, and several e-books.

Her speaking and writing career translated perfectly into other media, including hosting talk-shows on Christian radio, television, and voice-over work. Pamela earned a certificate in apologetics from Biola University. Her first passion is to help others in matters of faith. Her favorite pastimes are food, family, and friends. Weekends, when she's not speaking or writing, you'll find her cooking and entertaining—expressing her second passion for food, wine, and travel.

Pam and her husband live in Orange County, CA, with their two grown children and families living nearby. To book Pam to speak or to learn more, visit www.pamelachristianministries.com.

Get all the books in the

FAITH TO LIVE BY BOOK SERIES

Examine Your Faith!
Finding Truth in a World of Lies
(Revised 2015)

Renew Your Hope!
Remedy for Personal Breakthroughs
(Revised 2015)

Revive Your Life!
Rest for Your Anxious Heart
(2017)

To be sure you don't miss the release of all Pam's books, events and more, sign up for her bi-monthly newsletter.

www.pamelachristianministries.com
Pamela Christian Ministries
18032 Lemon Dr. #C206, Yorba Linda, CA 92886
info@pamelachristianministries.com

OTHER TITLES BY PAMELA CHRISTIAN:

First book in the Faith to Live By Book Series:

EXAMINE YOUR FAITH! FINDING TRUTH IN A WORLD OF LIES

Well-meaning people want to believe all roads lead to the same God and heaven. But wanting something to be true is far different from truth lining up with reality.

- What is truth?
- Is it relative or absolute?
- Is it personal or universal?
- What are the differences among the various religious faiths? Can they be blended?

This book will help you possess a confident faith that will sustain you in any life adversity.

Second book in the Faith to Live By Series:

RENEW YOUR HOPE! REMEDY FOR PERSONAL BREAKTHROUGHS

This book provides the answers that can change your life, your circumstances, and your future.

- Learn the fullness of what Christ offers you
- Uncover the deceptions that have prevented you from moving ahead
- Discover Christ's authority and power that God wants you to operate in
- Take hold of the abundant, victorious life Christ died to provide you

You can have confident hope. You can have personal breakthroughs. Why wait a moment longer when this book places the answers in your hands?

His Word Afresh, My Life Anew!

Those interested in the history and origin of the Bible and learning an inductive method for independent Bible study will enjoy this workbook. The A-F-R-E-S-H method allows in-depth and applied study of God's Word.

- **Paperback:** 86 pages
- **Language:** English
- **ISBN-10:** 1456541153
- **ISBN-13:** 978-1456541156

TO ORDER COPIES OF THIS OR ANY OF PAM'S BOOKS:

If you liked this book of Pam's, you'll like others to keep or to give as gifts. Order at the website www.pamelachristianminstries.com, or use this form to order by mail.

Name:____
First and Last

Shipping
Address:____
Street and Suite/Apartment number if applicable

____
City, State and Zip

Phone
Number:____
Area code and number

Email
Address:____

Please be sure to provide a phone or email address in case we have any question about the proper fulfillment of your order.

TITLE	RETAIL	QUANTITY	TOTAL
Examine Your Faith! Finding Truth in a World of Lies	$16.99	________	________
Examine Your Faith! Study Guide	$7.99	________	________
Renew Your Hope! Remedies for Personal Breakthroughs	$16.99	________	________
Renew Your Hope! Study Guide	$7.99	________	________
His Word Afresh, My Life Anew!	$11.99	________	________

TOTAL: $______

California residents add 8% tax $______

Add $3.00 postage for each book* $______

GRAND TOTAL: $______

Shipping limited to the United States

Please send this form with your check or money order payable to:
Pamela Christian Ministries
18032 Lemon Drive #C206
Yorba Linda, CA 92886